Songs in a Strange Land

The Psalms and Canticles Today

PATRICK RODGER

MOWBRAY

First published 1989
by Mowbray, a Cassell imprint,
Artillery House, Artillery Row,
London, SW1P 1RT

Typeset by Getset (BTS) Limited, Eynsham, Oxon.
Printed in Great Britain by Cox and Wyman Ltd, Reading.

British Library Cataloguing in Publication Data
Rodger, Patrick
Songs in a strange land: the psalms
and canticles today.
1. Bible, O.T. Psalms – Devotional
works
I. Title
242'.5

ISBN 0-264-67159-7

Dedication

MARGARITAE PRETIOSAE

Contents

Preface

On a winter afternoon the radio is on in the kitchen. As the work of the household goes forward, it is accompanied by one of the most beautiful sounds that the Anglican tradition can produce: a cathedral choir is chanting the Psalms for the day. Whether jubilant or plaintive, they seem to come from another world – and in a sense they do. For it may be that the listener does not much regard the words that are being sung. At best the sound may be a pleasing but fleeting aesthetic experience, in a generation which listens to famous Masses and other church music in concert halls rather than in churches. And even to the performers, for whom the Psalms are a part of their daily diet, there may yet be a remoteness about them. The choristers (to those who know choristers) will very soon have shed the sweet tones of Elizabethan English and will be talking of football and space invaders in their own dialect. Indeed, the clergy themselves may well be conducting the rest of their worship in a very different kind of language: the flat, wordy, unpoetic English of the late 20th century. Truly the Psalms are (perhaps with the exception of 'The Lord is my shepherd. . .' and 'All people that on earth do dwell. . .') songs in a strange land; and it would be quite surprising if it were not so, when one considers their antiquity of some three thousand years and the different context out of which they came. And yet Jews and Christians continue to sing, recite or read them in private. Despite the obvious difficulties and objections to the Psalms, which we shall be considering in the course of this book, their durable quality has been unsurpassed, and it will be a great part of my endeavour to consider why.

The Psalms have been traditionally ascribed to King David, 'the sweet singer of Israel' (just as Proverbs and other wisdom literature are ascribed to Solomon). Given the persistence of tradition in that which can be sung or recited, there is no reason to deny that some of the Psalms may indeed go back to David's authorship; but in this book I have followed the generality of modern scholars in thinking that the Psalter forms a collection of poems or hymns from different hands and dates, *e.g.* during or after the captivity in Babylon (604–538 B.C.). Hence my frequent reference to 'the Psalmists' in the plural. Yet the remarkable thing is that this collection of 150 poems of diverse origin does not leave the impression of a hotchpotch but has preserved a wonderful unity of feeling, rather as the artists and craftsmen of different centuries have contributed to the unity of some great cathedral.

I have pondered carefully the question whether to quote the Psalms in the Coverdale translation of the Book of Common Prayer or to use a modern version such as the Liturgical Psalter in The Alternative Service Book 1980. I have opted for the former, except in cases where the wording is either obscure or clearly incorrect: not (in spite of what was said above) because I am one of those who believe that God can be worshipped only in archaic language, but because my book is meditative in character, not a commentary which would require the pen of a Hebrew scholar. As an attempt to share the experience of using the Psalms, it must rely a good deal on the association of familiar wording, and this Coverdale still supplies for many English-speaking Christians, four hundred and fifty years after the publication of his 'Great Bible' in 1539.

There remains the question of how my book may best contribute to the Lenten study which is its object. It is primarily designed for those who may from time to time sing, or listen to, the Psalms in public worship but seldom read them in private, perhaps because they seem rather formal and alien. It may also be the case, however, that others who are thoroughly familiar with the words of the Psalms may find here some new approaches. In either case, I suggest that after a private reading of the Introduction and Chapter 1, it might be profitable to make a list of a few Psalms appropriate to Chapters 2–6 respectively – where a good number are quoted – and to read them afresh in the light of what I have written. You may also care in each week to take one or more canticles from the second half of this book, where the chapters are much shorter. The Psalms chosen might be your own favourite ones, or they might on the other hand be ones that you have always found difficult or even particularly disliked. For a part of our Lenten discipline may well be to come to grips with those things in our religious tradition that have never attracted us or spoken to our condition.

These are suggestions for personal use, but there is no reason why they should not apply to group study as well – provided that the members of the group are willing to do some reading in between their meetings (for it is the lack of such preparation that constitutes the weakness of many groups and allows them to degenerate into mere chit-chat). Bible study groups do not often, in my experience, devote themselves to the Old Testament, and this is a pity. The Psalms may furnish one of the easiest points of entry into the world of the Old Testament; and Christian people, some of whom may greatly love and value the Psalms and others who still feel 'in a strange land' with them, will each have his or her different viewpoint to contribute to the discussion and fellowship of the group.

Introduction: The Psalms and Christ's Prayer

The predominant values of worship today are, if I am not mistaken, honesty and simplicity. In a generation where each person is encouraged to try to discover and express his true self, *authenticity* is held to be of high importance. Let prayer and praise, however crude, however halting, be real for me! And indeed one may well sympathise with this desire. To many people, the traditional forms of worship, with their accompanying orthodoxies, now seem like a straitjacket which they are glad to cast aside. Thought-forms which are archaic, words which are barely intelligible, not to mention Anglican chants which provide musical hurdles for untrained congregations: all these may militate against a sympathetic approach to the Psalms, as indeed to many other books of the Bible. Let each pilgrim, it may be said, take to the road and find his own pace unhampered by so much heavy and old-fashioned luggage. The trouble, however, with a reliance upon one's personal resources alone is that one often comes so quickly to the end of them. In any art there is a natural desire in a beginner to establish his originality, 'to do his own thing'; but the casting aside of authority and tradition as oppressive forces generally reveals the nakedness of the land (save in the very rare case of genius). Until we go to school with this or that master of the art, we are usually no better than undisciplined amateurs, and it will not be long before we are depressed, not just by our lack of technique but by the poverty of our imagination. Is it not for this reason that many modern attempts at prayer in church are criticised as thin and second-rate? Yet this is not simply – as Anglicans so often assume – a question of language, of 'you' versus 'thou', and so on. It concerns the very *sources* of prayer, the well-springs without which there can be no flow at all.

We may be thankful, therefore, that the Christian is not left to his own devices. True, each has to find his or her particular way (and time) of prayer. We have Jesus' own encouragement to go in and **'shut the door and pray to our Father in secret'** – and not to suppose that we shall be heard through using a torrent of words, for our hearts and needs are already known to God (Matt. 6. 6–8). It is a wise saying that God wants you 'to pray as you can, not as you can't'. Yet even in our privacy we are not alone or unassisted. For first of all, it is the Holy Spirit, God himself, who prays within us, whether in words or simply **'with groanings that cannot be uttered'** (Rom. 8. 26). Moreover, we do not pray in spiritual isolation but always as members of a Body. *Communio sanctorum* may be translated as 'the communion of saints' or as 'the sharing in holy things', and both meanings are true. By the very act of praying, however inadequately, we join a company, and one which extends throughout space and time; it includes those for whom we intercede and who intercede for us, but far, far more who are personally unknown to us. For all are turned towards that centre from whom life, light and assistance radiate – and all, in Christian language, make their prayers 'through Jesus Christ our Lord', no empty formula as we shall see.

The fact that we pray, not only in church but in our own homes, out of doors or on a bed of sickness, as members of a great company, offers us two further pieces of encouragement. First, we may know (for they have often told us) that the saints have encountered just the same difficulties, doubts, periods of dryness and apathy, as we do in our own small way.

Once they were mourning here below
And wet their couch with tears;
They wrestled hard, as we do now
With sins and doubts and fears.

And if we are looking for confirmation of the truth of that verse, we shall find plenty in the Psalms for a start. Secondly, it is a source of strength and comfort to know that the very words we utter have formed the material of prayer for so many that have gone before us 'with the sign of faith' – that those same words have passed through so many minds and hearts before our own, linking us with God and with one another. Of no book is this more true than the Psalter. We may think of the Psalms as they originally were, poems based on Hebrew parallelism (the regular method of Hebrew poetry, whereby one verse expresses the same idea in two parallel forms, *e.g.* in Ps. 46: 'God is our hope and strength: a very present help in trouble. . . the Lord of hosts is with us: the God of Jacob is our refuge') – and to hear them read by a Jew, as was my good fortune once a year in the Cathedral at Oxford, is a moving experience in itself. We may think of them in the Latin of quaintly illuminated manuscripts from centuries ago; in the much-loved doggerel of the metrical versions which dominated Protestant worship for centuries after the Reformation; in this or that new translation into some Asian or African language. The Psalms have been the daily food of the Fathers of the Church, of the religious communities in all centuries, and also of many an ordinary priest and lay person. They transcend age, denomination, theological position, not least because they are so much older than most of our divisions and disagreements. If ever there was a common heritage for Jews and Christians to prize together, it is in the Psalter; and it is a heritage not just to admire but to use. Here is one of the oldest manuals of worship in the world – over 2,000 years in continuous use, as the advertisement might say.

It remains, however, a question for the Christian as to how he makes that manual his own, and here the nub must be whether he finds Christ in this book of pre-Christian worship. I do not refer only to those Psalms which to the early Church (and perhaps to Jesus himself) were taken as clearly predictive of his suffering and of his glory as Messiah, but to the Psalter as a whole. As we read these poetic prayers, with their great variations of mood and approach to God, it is necessary that we should have some criterion for assessing their value to our own spirits. Again, it is inevitable that this should be to some extent the outlook of our own time and place: a child of a scientific and sceptical generation does not read any part of the Bible just as a medieval monk, or even a Victorian believer, would have done. Yet this is not the only, or the most important, criterion that we are called upon to employ; for, as has been said, it may soon bring us to the limits of our own small spiritual experience and give us a very provincial view of the riches of the past. The Body of Christ has been given the Mind of Christ, as St Paul was fond of reminding his readers, and it is to the discernment of that Mind that we must give our attention in using the Psalter.

The appeal of the Psalms lies first in their obvious and uninhibited humanity. They are, in the language of modern journalism, 'an intensely human document'. We need not on that account be afraid of associating them with the Son of Man and with the intimacy of his prayer to the Father, indeed, with that agony of which we have only occasional glimpses in the Gospels. We have enough evidence to suggest that Jesus loved and used the Psalms of his people Israel. Yet there is more to it than that, and for that 'more' we need to turn and consider for a little the fundamental Christian view of prayer. For this view dissents sharply from the widespread modern assumption that prayer is simply a part of what is called 'man's search for God' – who may or may not be there, and if perchance he is not, prayer is then at least a form of psychotherapy. The Psalms may be fitted into this category with deceptive ease. I say 'deceptive' because the Psalmists are not concerned only with man's search for God but with God's prior action in creation and redemption, or what theologians call his prevenience. **'In the beginning, God'**; and it is the development, or filling out, of that theme in Christianity which gives us our starting point.

'Man does not originate prayer, he joins in it.' I heard that saying many years ago at college and have found it a very present help ever since in the lifelong struggle of prayer. For prayer (and more especially praise and thanksgiving which are hard to describe as 'talking to oneself') belong within a relationship. And to the Christian that relationship is held to be eternally present within God the Holy Trinity. It is to that living relationship with his Father that Jesus Christ our representative – 'the proper man', in Martin Luther's phrase – has taken the prayer of humanity. The writer of the Epistle to the Hebrews gives the most famous expression to that belief: **'he ever lives to make intercession for us'** (Heb. 7.25). It is from this eternal priestly work of the Son on behalf of all humanity and all creation that our own small priesthood – the priesthood of the Church – receives its meaning and its motive power. Mother Teresa has put it in this way:

> In reality, there is only one true prayer, only one substantial prayer: Christ himself. There is only one voice which rises above the face of the earth: the

voice of Christ. His voice reunites and co-ordinates in itself all the voices raised in prayer.' (*Jesus, the Word to be Spoken*, p. 4, Collins, 1987)

Next we may call in evidence the Farewell Discourses of Jesus in St John's Gospel, where a close connection is made between that habit of prayer to which Jesus urges his disciples and his own continuing prayer to the Father, as a part of their living relationship which death cannot destroy:

> **And I will pray the Father, and he will give you another to be your Standby – the Spirit of Truth.(Jn 14.16)**

This same notion of praying in, or with the help of, the Holy Spirit is powerfully expressed by St Paul in a famous passage:

> **In the same way the Spirit comes to the aid of our weakness. We do not even know how we ought to pray, but through our inarticulate groans the Spirit himself is pleading for us, and God who searches our inmost being knows what the Spirit means because he pleads for God's people in God's own way(Rom. 8.26–27)**

Thus the Holy Spirit provides us with a language for our own prayers. It need not be 'speaking in a tongue', nor the language of tradition, nor yet our own eloquence. It may simply be the wordless intention of our longing (**'like as the hart desireth the waterbrooks. . .'** Ps. 42.1). God knows what it means because the Spirit of Christ, our eternal high priest and intercessor, is always there to help us.

Faith in this promise can be immensely liberating. It sets us free from that verbosity in prayer which in spite of the warning of Jesus seems to thrive today in many of our churches and house groups, perhaps in order to keep up with the television or the duplicated paper. But more profoundly such faith can free us from self-centredness, whether this is of the self-satisfied kind (of an accomplished liturgical performer) or, more often, of the nervous kind that is always wondering how the speaker is getting on with his prayers and why they have to be so dull and repetitive, and why they seem so much worse than those of other people (as if we knew), and how God must think very poorly of our efforts, *etc. etc.* When we have realised that our own little rivulet is simply one of thousands of tributaries flowing into that unfailing and majestic river which is Christ's prayer for us all, we may get things into a truer proportion and smile at our own small fuss and anxiety.

To rest upon the prayer of the Church, in the Psalter and elsewhere, at times when we are tired or drained of feeling or out of tune with the world and ourselves: this is a familiar experience for many members of the Body and a deeply welcome one. We join in common prayer at the Offices or the Eucharist and are borne along by it, sometimes not without a struggle. Nor is this mere community singing. To describe such prayer only as 'the prayer of the Church' may lead us into formalism and substitute a communal staleness of spirit for a personal one. No, the prayer of the Church is first of all *Christ's* prayer. It involves our joining not only with angels and archangels and all the company of heaven and earth but with the Lord and Mediator himself; so that (to take the most obvious example) every time we say the Lord's Prayer, the simplest and most hackneyed of all, we are saying it not only *after* the Lord, or *for* the Lord, but *with* the Lord. We are joining in what St Benedict truly called *opus Dei*, the work of God, that great enterprise of his Kingdom which sustains everyone and everything that he has made and which saves it all from crashing to the floor.

Such a faith is both uplifting and enriching but, of course, it does not let us off the hook. On the contrary! The mandate of Jesus was to persevere in prayer and never give up, for God (unlike man) likes the importunate. The teachers of the Church add to this their own testimony. 'Never give up praying, some day the miracle will happen,' said Abbé Paul Couturier of the Church's unity. We may not therefore plead that we are really no good at prayer, that it is not our scene. As in the musical context, one may have a voice like a corncrake, but that does not mean that the musical offering of the Church is either going to cease or to be left to the choral professionals only! No, each one is needed in that choir. The army of the Lord is not so numerous that any private soldier, however clumsy, can be spared. For it is not the unlikely development of each and every Christian into a virtuoso that is required; it is simply the connection, or plugging in, to that eternal prayer of adoration and thanksgiving, of intercession for humanity and all God's creatures which forms the *opus Dei*: and for that work, nothing but patience, humility and love will suffice.

We are often disposed to think about the quantity of our prayers, rather like the parish priest anxiously counting heads in the congregation; but, of course, their quantity is of little significance when compared with their quality. The Prayer Book was perhaps more conscious of this need than most of our modern liturgies:

> Let thy merciful ears, O Lord, be open to the prayers of thy humble servants: and that they may obtain their petitions, make them to ask such things as shall please thee. . . (Collect for Trinity 10)

If our prayers are indeed to keep company with those of Christ himself, there must a constant refinement of them – and this does not mean, as is sometimes supposed, just a refinement into beautiful Jacobean English (which would disqualify a good many of God's less poetic children) but a refinement of the *intention* of prayer, but public and private. For if there is a case for prayer which is altogether spontaneous, there is also a case for prayer which begins only after careful thought, or perhaps after certain actions have been taken. I am reminded of Alan Ecclestone's book *Yes to God*, in which he often speaks of our preparing ourselves in various ways – intellectual, practical, spiritual – for prayer. On reading that book, I realised how often I had blundered too hastily into speech and had failed to take off my shoes before entering on to holy ground.

In this opening chapter we may seem to have strayed far from the Psalms, but I do not believe it to be so: first, because these thoughts bear on a Christian use of the Psalms, but also, as it seems to me, because in the Psalms themselves there is a constant awareness of the unworthiness of the one who prays, coupled with a joyful dependence upon the God who hears and understands.

> **Teach me to do the thing that pleases thee, for thou art my God: let thy loving spirit lead me forth into the land of righteousness. (Ps. 143.10)**

The frequent appeals for victory and imprecations upon the enemy which, to our minds today, disfigure the Psalms may be no better or worse than the discordant prayers of 20th century Christians asking for the triumph of *their* national cause. Yet even they may, negatively as it were, point us to the truth. Prayer as the expression of our own wills or, worse still, of our own opinions, is a counterfeit of the real thing, and even the unbelieving world can recognise it as such. Jesus showed us its proper nature, which is the seeking of our Father's will in order to join in his great enterprise for all that He has made. We need not doubt that this was hard for Jesus. It called for his death and resurrection, and how many lesser deaths and resurrections is it likely to involve for us along the way! The struggle with self, which surfaces in many of the greatest Psalms, never ceases. Yet there is also present in them the conviction which Jesus developed to the full, that 'in His will is our peace', and indeed our unity as well; for once our voices cease to compete and join that of Christ himself, the harmony is immediate. And even along the way, and long before we have attained to the real depth of what prayer is, we may have glimpses of that vision and hear snatches of that harmony, and thus be enabled to persevere.

Seven Meditations on the Psalms

1
Alone and Together with the Psalms

One of the enduring characteristics of the Psalms is that they can be, and are, used both in public and in private. This qualifies them for the category of great music, great drama, and great literature; for it is the essence of these that they can be used, reflected on and enjoyed both when we are alone and when we are together with many others. It is not so with all art. Most of us have private tastes which we could not reasonably expect a company to enjoy (there are also tastes that we grow out of and some which last only for a limited period of our lives). On the other hand, there are works which in the excitement of an opera house or a concert hall would give us pleasure, but which we should find hard to listen to in our own homes. Similarly, there are pictures which we greatly admire in a gallery, but would certainly not wish to have hanging on our own walls. The experience of religion is comparable: there are prayers quite precious to ourselves but strictly for private consumption, and there are rites and ceremonies which require a full church to give them their proper meaning. The test, however, of that which is most authentic in worship is that it should be capable of use in either place, the sickroom or the cathedral. In the tradition of Judaism and Christianity, many parts of scripture may claim to pass that test, but none more so than the Psalms.

Stand in awe and sin not: commune with your own heart in your chamber, and be still. (Ps. 4.4)

O Lord, thou hast searched me out and known me: thou knowest my down-sitting and mine up-rising; thou understandest my thoughts long before. (Ps. 139.1)

but also:

. . . for I went with the multitude and brought them forth into the house of God, in the voice of praise and thanksgiving among such as keep holy-day. (Ps. 42.4)

O praise God in his holiness . . . let everything that hath breath praise the Lord. (Ps. 150.1,6)

Within the compass of these 150 poems are to be found the most intimate and uninhibited expressions of what we nowadays call 'personal religion', yet they are at the same time full of the sense of corporate worship. In church use they are saved again and again from mere formalism by the poignancy of the first person singular within them – while the priest reciting them alone in his daily office, and tempted perhaps by their familiarity to yield to boredom and staleness, is for ever being reminded of that company to whom they, and he, belong.

In our own day this combination may seem something of a paradox. For we live at a time when there is a real danger of personal religion being divorced altogether from corporate worship and, as they say, privatised. On the one hand, there are impressive religious occasions in great buildings witnessed, either in the flesh or on television, by many people who do not themselves pray. Indeed, there may well be a certain number of churchgoers who neither pray nor open the Bible between one Sunday and the next. On the other hand, researchers tell us that there are many people in our country who both read and pray at home and (as the old Scotsman said) 'scutter away with their souls by themselves', without ever joining in public worship. It may be revealing that we speak so much nowadays of 'community' and 'fellowship' in the Church – revealing of the fact that these things are rare and hard to come by in the world which we inhabit.

If this picture has truth in it, then the Psalms can do much to fortify our spiritual balance. They do so by drawing us into a relation between individual, church and nation, which is quite different from that to which we are accustomed. For the idea of private devotion, in the sense that the user might have nothing to do with a worshipping community, would have been quite strange to ancient Israel. The words 'I' and 'my' are, of course, extremely common in the Psalms but they are not to be understood as being, in our sense, individualistic. They might well have been uttered in the Temple, just as 'I believe in one God. . .' has traditionally been said by Christians in their public recitation of the Creed. In the same way we have grown accustomed to thinking of the Old Testament prophets as lonely and often unpopular figures. We have instances in the book of Jeremiah, above all, of the prophet's private communings – arguments might be a better word – with God. Yet the *content* of prophecy had always to do with the people of God, for better or for worse. The prophet lived among the people and was sent to speak to them; there is never any suggestion that for him religion is only a private exercise.

When, therefore, we speak of the Psalter as 'the hymn book of the Church', we are making no division between the corporate and the personal, since the Church is as truly present in its members in dispersion as in their assembling together. And it is interesting that this hymn book has been even more thoroughly used in public by the Christian Church than by its Jewish progenitor. According to

W.O.E. Oesterley, the scholar and historian of the Psalter, only about half the Psalms were regarded as suitable for worship in the Temple, and this is still true of the Synagogue today – whereas the Church, for most of its life, has swallowed them whole. At any rate, as early as 494 A.D. the Patriarch of Constantinople refused to ordain anyone who could not recite the whole Psalter off by heart (a rule that might drastically reduce the demand for ordination, both male and female, in our own day). From the writings of the Fathers it is evident that the early Church had already 'gone overboard' for the Psalms, but it is probably their use in the monastic tradition which has been most influential of all in making them part of the staple diet of our public worship. In the mediaeval Service Books for the Hours the entire Psalter was ordered to be read in the course of a week. In the Book of Common Prayer it is covered in a month. Modern service books are more sparing still in their distribution of the Psalms, and it may be that this is a wiser policy from the point of view of their absorption by congregations. Any regular routine which includes the whole Psalter will avoid the danger of sticking to a few well-worn favourites and thus missing the true richness and balance of the whole. Whatever the practice of any particular generation or Church, it can be claimed that the Christian soul has always been steeped in the Psalms hitherto.

There is more to be said, however, about the difference between the perspective of the Old Testament and our own. When reading the Psalms in private, we may remember that we do so as those who belong to the Church; but it would be unlikely to occur to us that we do so as those who belong to a wider community, *viz.* the whole nation. To the Psalmists, on the contrary, the Church *was* the nation, God's people of Israel whether faithful or backsliding, and the nation the Church. This constant sense of solidarity between the individual and the whole people, good and bad alike, permeates the Law, the Prophets and the Psalms, and constitutes one of the best reasons for our not losing the reading of the Old Testament. It is by no means easy to think ourselves back into that world, or even the world of three or four hundred years ago in our own country, and thus recapture the sense of our religious solidarity with the whole community. For the idea of a Church detached from the community, as of a believer detached from the Church, has gained a great deal of ground among modern Christians – it is the very hallmark of denominations living in a pluralist society. This in itself could well make the Psalms appear to us like 'songs in a strange land'.

Yet there is another kind of help for us in the realisation that the Psalter, in spite of its associations with chanting, choir stalls, antiphonal recitation and all the rest of it, is not at all a narrowly ecclesiastical book. Its wide dimensions will occupy the rest of these pages. The challenge for us, therefore, is to think how the Psalms apply even to the life of a secularised and seemingly indifferent society like our own. Is the right way to approach that question an identification of ourselves with the virtuous minority, and of 'outsiders' with the wicked or the fools who say in their hearts that there is no God (Ps. 14.1)? Certainly some of the Psalms could be taken as lending support to that comfortably sectarian spirit – and yet there is also to be found in others a universal claim upon every one of God's creatures to give him thanks and praise. And it is that universal claim which, as we shall see, is taken up and fulfilled by Jesus Christ and made binding upon the Christian.

* * *

What then is the attitude of the Psalms to the community of which the singer forms part? Its foundation is that a man cannot love God and remain indifferent to his neighbour and his doings. In other words, it is in accord both with the Law of Moses and with the subsequent teaching of the New Testament. There are, of course, a great many passages in the Psalms which speak of a community – international, national or local – which is disordered and hostile. The writer thinks of himself as on his own; he seeks God as a refuge, a court of appeal, a hiding-place from human behaviour. For even the so-called neighbour turns out to be a treacherous enemy and this does not simply apply to the surrounding nations which threaten Israel, but to parties within Israel itself, to families and friends.

> **. . . even mine own familiar friend whom I trusted, who did also eat of my bread, hath laid great wait for me.** (Ps. 41.9)

> **My lovers and friends hast thou put away from me and hid mine acquaintance out of my sight.**
> (Ps. 88.18)

Thus the Psalmists are never guilty of idealising the community or erecting it into an idol called 'the people', in the foolish and often hypocritical way that 20th century nation states have been apt to do. Having a grimly realistic estimate of human nature, collectively as well as individually, they know that one's relations with others are often fickle, untrustworthy and dangerous, and that there can be no substitute for a reliance on the unchanging faithfulness of God Himself. So for the God-fearing it is written:

> **Thou shalt hide them privily by thine own presence from the provoking of all men: thou shalt keep them secretly in thy tabernacle from the strife of tongues.**
> (Ps. 31.21)

(A very necessary and reassuring verse in days when the media are apt to hold sway.)

The mood of the Psalms, however, is by no means always one of isolation and alienation. There is also pleasure to be found in human society, especially that of fellow pilgrims and fellow-worshippers. This is most marked in the series of short Psalms, 120 onwards, known as the Songs of Ascents (were they short because you needed plenty of breath to walk uphill towards Jerusalem?)

> **For my brethren and companions' sakes I will wish thee prosperity; yea, because of the house of the Lord I will seek to do thee good.** (Ps. 122.8–9)

There is even (though it is rare) some celebration in Psalms 127 and 128 of the joys of marriage, home and children. And, of course, the characteristic Jewish note that our immortality lies in our posterity is struck again and again by the Psalmists. Nothing could be better in human life than to see your descendants growing up – and every grandparent will feel an echo of these sentiments in his or her own heart.

> **The Lord from out of Sion shall so bless thee that thou shalt see Jerusalem in prosperity all thy life long. Yea, that thou shalt see thy children's children and peace upon Israel.** (Ps. 128.6–7)

As for the working life of man, it is only glanced at in a few Psalms, most memorably in the great nature Psalm 104 and in Psalm 107.

> **O Lord, how manifold are thy works: in wisdom has thou made them all; the earth is full of thy riches!**(Ps. 104.24)

Within this good creation, it is chiefly the dependence of man upon his creator that is being rehearsed – the chief joy of the sailor is when he manages to get safely into port (Ps. 107.30)! The general picture is that we are blessed when we are in harmony with our environment, **'in league with the stones of the field'** in Job's vivid phrase (Job 5. 23), and like the animals and the fruits of the earth are answering the divine intention and thus fulfilling our own nature. Are these not thoughts which are recurring forcibly to our own generation, as we begin to doubt our arrogant claims to independence and to be afraid of the consequences of human greed and general disharmony with a nature which we have violated? Harvest Thanksgiving has for many years been regarded as an occasion (often an isolated one) of nostalgia for older ways before the supermarket had replaced the fields and the trees for most worshippers. But while the Psalms, notably 65, 67 and 145, may be traditionally associated with the joy of harvest, the concern of the Psalter with nature is much wider than that; for the whole world of creatures, both animate and inanimate (in which Jesus himself rejoiced), is at once the frame of our lives and the sphere of our responsibility. It is for this reason that the chorus of praise rendered to the Creator (to which we shall next turn) extends far beyond the human community and takes in everything that he has made.

> **Let the heavens rejoice, and let the earth be glad: let the sea make a noise, and all that therein is. Let the field be joyful and all that is in it: then shall the trees of the wood rejoice before the Lord. For he cometh, he cometh to judge the earth: and with righteousness to judge the world, and the people with his truth.**
>
> **(Ps. 96.11–13)**

2
Making a Joyful Noise

There is only one possible place from which to start on the content of the Psalms and that is praise and thanksgiving. For there is hardly a single Psalm, even among the most anguished or lachrymose, which does not contain at least one or two verses of straight praise. The whole book is a manual of doxology, the telling of glory. It is this God-directed character of the Psalms which gives them their particular flavour. If, like many modern people, even churchgoing ones, you have little taste for transcendence or the God who is above heaven and earth, the Psalms will again seem like songs in a strange land – but they will not lose their challenge or their fascination. For they address us with a passion which can sweep us off our cautious feet. It is no faint praise in which they indulge: the heart dances for joy, sometimes even in the most unfavourable of circumstances, the instruments are exhorted to tune up and give of their best, and we too are invited to sing with gusto and join the great congregation *fortissimo*.

> **It is a good thing to give thanks unto the Lord, and to sing praises unto thy Name, O most Highest; to tell of thy loving-kindness early in the morning and of thy truth in the night season; upon an instrument of ten strings and upon the lute, upon a loud instrument and upon the harp. For thou, Lord, hast made me glad through thy works: and I will rejoice in giving praise for the operations of thy hands. (Ps. 92.1–4)**

'It is a good thing' because in the rendering of praise we are fulfilling the nature with which we and our fellow creatures were endowed from the beginning – **'when the morning stars sang together and all the sons of God shouted for joy'** (Job 38.7). Here is a place where deep instinct is combined with the highest skill of which humanity is capable; for while our response to the glory of God 'in the operations of his hands' is a spontaneous one, it also summons up the greatest resources of our own creative powers in art, music and literature, and even then knows that the glory is past expression. In the Christian tradition, there may be some distance, aesthetically speaking, between a motet sung by a Cathedral choir and *Songs of Praise* belting it out on a beach one Sunday evening; but they belong to the same family. The Psalms and the Canticles (to which we shall return in the second part of this book) are the patriarchs of that family, and there is already in them a sufficient range of feeling to encourage us in thinking that there are many ways of praising God and that we should not hastily condemn the ways of others as 'vulgar' or 'precious' or whatever. What the family has in common is the capacity to respond joyfully to the love of its origin –

> O for a thousand tongues to sing
> My dear Redeemer's praise!

It is necessary here, however, to pause and consider an objection. Does it jar on you, all this banging on the drum and shaking the timbrel like a Salvation Army band? In his book *Reflections on the Psalms*, C.S. Lewis has a chapter called 'A Word about Praising', in which he says that when Christianity first came alive for him, he was dismayed by this ceaseless emphasis on praise. Does God, he asked himself, really demand this kind of everlasting eulogy; and if so, what manner of vain autocrat can He be? The question was understandable when we recall the sickening flattery of the dictators of our own century, men who for the most part were being 're-assessed' and often reviled quite soon after they were dead. But, says Lewis, he came to see that as far as the Psalms were concerned, he was viewing the matter the wrong way round. It was not a matter of God exacting praise on pain of some penalty or other – it was the inevitable response of human nature at its healthiest to the glory of God. Here are his words:

> I had never noticed that all enjoyment spontaneously overflows into praise unless (sometimes even if) shyness or the fear of boring others is deliberately brought in to check it. The world rings with praise – lovers praising their mistresses, readers their favourite poet, walkers praising the countryside, players praising their favourite game – praise of weather, winds, dishes, actors, motors, horses, colleges, countries, historical personages, children, flowers, mountains, rare stamps, rare beetles, even sometimes politicians or scholars. I had not noticed how the humblest and at the same time most balanced and capacious minds praised most, while the cranks, misfits and malcontents praised least.
> (Reflections on the Psalms: Bles, 1958, p. 94.)

Lewis's words are even more to the point than when he wrote them thirty years ago, for we have advanced further into an age which is for the most part anxious, critical, analytical and self-centred. In the atmosphere of our present culture, to indulge in uninhibited praise of anything, be it a person or a thing, is very likely to be accused of being 'naïve' – the ultimate offence to the sophisticated mind! If you go overboard for anyone or anything, you are immediately exposed to the danger of making a fool of yourself and of committing yourself to a judgement which you may subsequently regret. And indeed that *is* the risk which enthusiasm is bound to run (nor are the Psalmists so naïve as to be altogether unaware of that risk; they do from time to time ponder as to whether their praise of God could have been misplaced). At any rate, praise is the shortest road to self-forgetfulness. To revert to that programme of hymnody already mentioned, *Songs of Praise*, its significance lies not so much in the quality of the hymns chosen as in the fact that such numbers of people, both singers and viewers, are still prepared to be 'lost in wonder, love and praise'. It was an agreeable surprise to hear a critic on another programme describe *Songs of Praise* as 'an oasis of goodness' in the modern world and its television. If you believe that the world is sick and faint for want of a sense of glory in God and man, you will like that description. For it is the nature of an oasis to centre round water, a commodity which we do not produce for ourselves but discover and tap, hoping that it will prove an inexhaustible resource.

Some modern theologians have maintained that 'God' is simply shorthand for the religious principle within the self. If you hold this, it is difficult to see how you can make sense of the Psalms, or avoid saying that they are out of date. For one can hardly imagine praise being addressed – and addressed with such emphasis and enthusiasm – to the religious principle within oneself without producing an intolerable degree of self-satisfaction. (Perhaps, alas, that very thing may be detected in certain church choirs, not to mention certain clergy!) But the theology on which the Psalms are based is, of course, altogether different. It assumes a Deity who regularly addresses his creatures and who in turn can be addressed by them, since they are passionately involved with one another. We speak in this chapter of praise and thanksgiving, but it should be remembered that the Psalmists sometimes address God in other and sharper tones. Like Job they are not afraid to question and even reproach the Lord of the universe.

> **Up, Lord, why sleepest thou? Awake and be not absent from us for ever.** (Ps. 44.23)

or in the most famous reproach of all –

> **My God, my God, look upon me, why hast thou forsaken me? and art so far from my health and from the words of my complaint.** (Ps. 22.1)

There is never any doubt in the Psalms that there is indeed a God 'out there', the living God who speaks, acts, rewards, punishes, can be celebrated, neglected, or insulted; and that there is a constant dialogue – sometimes an argument or controversy – between the Lord and his people. For this living God is the God of Israel, the One who has already spoken and acted in particular events of history, which are to be constantly rehearsed by his thankful people from generation to generation and remembered even when they are in the lowest pit of adversity.

* * *

It is now time to ask how it stands today with the praise and thanksgiving of modern Christians. To start with, if the instinct for praise is something general in human nature as God has made it, we do not need to be snobbish or exclusive in our claims. In particular, we have inherited the Psalms from the Jews and still share that treasure with them. But we must go on to ask how the use of the Psalms is affected by God's revealing of himself in his Son. In the New Testament we find repeated certain verses which the early Church used as *testimonia*, or witness-texts, to Christ as Messiah:

The Lord said to my Lord, Sit on my right hand till I make thine enemies thy footstool. (Ps. 110.1; see Mk. 12. 36, Acts 2.35 *etc.*)

Thou wilt not leave my soul in hell, nor suffer thy Holy One to see corruption. (Ps. 16.10; see Acts 2.27, 13.35)

The same stone which the builders refused has become the headstone of the corner. This is the Lord's doing, and it is marvellous in our eyes. (Ps. 118.22–23; see Mk. 12.10, 1 Pet. 2.7 *etc.*)

These are the favourite texts, but in the Letters of St Paul and the Letter to the Hebrews, the application of the Psalms to Jesus Christ goes much wider. They form a vital part of that Scripture which he said he had come not to destroy but to fulfil. Our reading of the Psalms, therefore, like the old page-headings of the Bible, is shot through with his presence. Indeed, we may well say that there are a good many Psalms which we can only recite in sincerity and truth because we are referring them not to our own experience but to his. In sorrow or in joy, there is in them a purity of intention towards God which few of us could claim save in rare moments, but which become altogether appropriate when the lips of Jesus utter them for us:

O God, thou art my God, early will I seek thee. My soul thirsteth for thee, my flesh also longeth after thee, in a barren and dry land where no water is. (Ps. 63.1).

Why art thou so heavy, O my soul, and why art thou so disquieted within me? O put thy trust in God, for I will yet give him thanks, which is the help of my countenance and my God. (Ps. 43.5–6)

Like the rest of our prayer to the Father, we read such verses 'through Jesus Christ our Lord'.

On the other hand, there are some features of the Psalms which can only drop away when Christ has come. We shall look at these in the next chapter. What remains, above all, is their God-directedness and intimacy of feeling. To his disciples, Jesus spoke of the naturalness of communion with their Father in heaven, both when they were together and when alone behind closed doors. It is in his Spirit that so many of the Psalms still have a profound meaning for us today.

> **I will give thanks unto the Lord with my whole heart, secretly among the faithful and in the congregation. The works of the Lord are great, sought out of all them that have pleasure therein.** (Ps. 111.1–2)

But there is more. For it is also true of the Psalms that, as originally written, they contain a large element of the tragic which they cannot always turn into praise. One thinks especially of the many references to death, as that Pit from which no man returns and from which he can no longer praise God. The Psalms resemble the classical literature of Greece and Rome in their poignant references to the brevity of human life.

> **The days of man are but as grass, for he flourisheth as a flower of the field. For as soon as the wind goeth over it, it is gone: and the place thereof shall know it no more.** (Ps. 103.15–16)

And then there are abundant references to ills which may be less final than death but are still overwhelming; humiliation, defeat, persecution, sickness, loneliness, misery, are all vividly brought before us. To say that we have risen above all these or been rendered immune to them because we are Christians would be palpably untrue – if we had, we should have lost our humanity. Which of us who has ever conducted or attended a funeral does not know the deep resonance of some of those universal Psalms?

Our own age is probably second to none in its expression – through the works of many artists, writers and composers – of the misery and apparent futility of much human existence. There is a fellow-feeling with such experiences in many of the Psalmists. If the predominant notes are those of joy and praise, assuredly there is nothing superficial about them; nor can there be for any who have entered in any degree into the suffering and abandonment of the crucified Jesus. For Christians, while reading the words of many Psalms as prophetic, believe that their sorrow and their joy have alike found fulfilment in the Word made flesh.

We read the Psalms as the people of the Cross and Resurrection of Jesus Christ, believing that through his trust in God and his love for God's creatures he attained to a life that could never be destroyed and made us partakers of that risen life; so that we are able to say that the experience of the human condition portrayed in the Psalms has been redeemed by Christ. It is therefore possible – and not only possible but right, *dignum et justum est* – for us his people to give praise and thanksgiving to God in a way that even the Psalmists could not do. Their hallowed words are used to go beyond their original sense, in order to celebrate the victory of the Lord over evil and death, and everything which has flowed ever since from that victory. What scholars call the typological use of the Psalms (roughly, using Old Testament words in a New Testament sense) may sound dull enough, but there is nothing dull about it at Eastertide!

When Israel came out of Egypt and the house of Jacob from among the strange people, Judah was his sanctuary and Israel his dominion. The sea saw that and fled: Jordan was driven back. (Ps. 114.1–3)

The turning of lamentation into joy is a familiar enough theme in the Psalms, as it is in the Prophets. It remains for the Christian to affirm that such a transformation does not depend upon fortune or emotion, but results from the irreversible act of God himself who raised Jesus from the dead.

> **When the Lord turned again the captivity of Sion, then were we like unto them that dream. Then was our mouth filled with laughter and our tongue with joy.** (Ps. 126.1–2)

3
Some Objections Considered

Thus far we have spoken of the Psalms with almost unstinted praise, but of course it is not all plain sailing. There are certain objections which occur easily to the mind of the modern reader (including, but not only, the Christian reader) as he contemplates the Psalms. It seems sensible, therefore, as well as honest to meet some of these objections head on and not leave them as so many disloyal thoughts lurking in the background. Nothing is more harmful to the study of the Bible as a whole than the combination of an outward reverence which would treat it as a 'sacred cow' beyond criticism, and a secret *arrière-pensée* that much of it is either untrue or irrelevant. Such an attitude is by no means uncommon today, and it constitutes a real hindrance to an intelligent faith.

The first objection is obvious enough and has been frequently voiced. It is that the Psalms are liberally peppered with references to the writer's enemies, to the wicked and ungodly who appear to flourish in large numbers. There are accompanying prayers, of great frequency and urgency, that God would deliver and avenge his servants and correspondingly defeat, destroy, or at least humiliate their enemies, **'smiting them in the hinder parts and putting them to a perpetual shame'** (Ps. 78.67). Even if we omit those sections generally known as 'the cursing Psalms' which our modern prayer books have bracketed, there are still many passages which cry out of a beleaguered state for deliverance from cruel foes – and upon these let the God of Israel show no mercy!

Now we might well have felt that such verses had not gone out of date if we had been Jews living under a Nazi régime or in a Soviet prison in recent years, or perhaps just Israelis feeling threatened by hostile neighbouring states. One may naturally think of the strutting Fascists, 'their eyes swelling with fatness', as one reads the anguished petitions of the persecuted and oppressed. Indeed, one may grimly admit that such passages in the Psalms have acquired a new lease of life in our violent and blood-stained century. Yet for those of us whose lives have been relatively peaceful, the problem remains. We should be exceptionally unfortunate if we had that number of enemies and suffered that degree of injustice and ill-treatment in our own experience. Thus it may well seem to us unhealthy as well as artificial to read the Psalms in their literal sense. We may from time to time conceive a hatred against an employer, a government department, a certain newspaper, even the representatives of a particular church, but our religion should surely not encourage us to maintain such a vindictive spirit against them.

For this reason, it was for a long time part of the Christian tradition to interpret such passages *allegorically* (in the style, *e.g.* of *Pilgrim's Progress*, one of the greatest allegories in the English language), and so to internalise the conflicts about which they spoke. It was then the hidden enemies of the soul who were in the reader's mind.

> **For we wrestle not against flesh and blood, but against principalities and powers and spiritual wickedness in high places. (Eph. 6.12)**

There is evident value in this recognition by the Christian that the age-old tendency to objectify God's enemies – as the Muslims, the Communists or whoever it may be – is a perversion of the Gospel he has received, and that the power of evil which has constantly to be resisted is as much within him as outside. For those who can interpret the Psalms in such a way it may be a fruitful method. I can only say that I cannot do it at all naturally or at any rate with any consistency, and I suspect that an age like ours which is deeply interested in outward event and historical context has little aptitude for allegorising.

There is, however, another approach to such passages which is neither literal nor allegorical with reference to ourselves, but rather *Christological.* Here we are reciting the Psalms first and foremost with the experience of Jesus himself in mind. The clearest examples are to be found in those Psalms of the Passion as they are called (22 and 69 in particular), to which we shall return in chapter 6. But there are many other Psalms which we may associate not only with Jesus' trust and joy in his Father's love but also with his acute sense of loneliness, betrayal by friends, and sharp trial of faith. To any Christian there is deep truth in this approach, and it will lead us into the whole matter of reading the Psalms in the light of the Messiah whom we confess.

This does not relieve us of our original difficulty with those Psalms which breathe a spirit of implacable hatred and desire for vengeance. Indeed, it intensifies the difficulty, for how can we read such words in the name of him who prayed on the Cross '**Father, forgive them, for they know not what they do**'? It looks as if the only remedy were to write off considerable sections of the Psalter as belonging both to a pre-Christian era and a non-Christian mentality. And yet the age-old instinct of the Church that it would be wrong to bowdlerise the Psalms as drastically as that was surely sound. For to do that would be to rob those old poems (as so many other books of the Old Testament) of their authenticity, and to present their human nature and ours as something other than it really is. To reduce the Psalms to that which is invariably edifying and perfect would be as great a falsehood as a similar reduction of the parables of Jesus who '**knew what was in man**' and portrayed human life as it is, not always as it ought to be. It would make the Psalms far less able to act as genuine vehicles of the human heart, that heart which always needs healing and reconciliation. For while we may not be able to identify our enemies as simply as the Psalmists did, we recognise ourselves sometimes (and with much less external cause) to be just as full of anger, bitterness, resentment, despair, and indignation against God and man, as those honest writers of old. Would not our religion be seriously deficient if it could not bring such dark and bitter feelings to the surface, where they might feel the touch of Christ who banished the evil spirits from humanity? Already in the Psalms we find the beginning of such a prayer, to the God who alone knows the heart's anguish and alone can rescue it from sinking deeper into the black waters –

> **He brought me also out of the horrible pit, out of the mire and clay, and set my feet upon the rock and ordered my goings. And he hath put a new song in my mouth, even a thanksgiving unto our God.**
>
> **(Ps. 40.2–3)**

The second objection to the Psalms is the converse of the first, but less frequently observed. It refers to a mood of self-satisfaction in the writers which most of us today are apt to find repugnant. In a good many Psalms (the most notable and lengthy example being Ps. 119) it is assumed that the writer is a virtuous character, well assured that God is on his side and that he is therefore entitled to judge and condemn others. This is what has been called the 'what a good boy am I!' syndrome, and to the modern reader it is probably as unattractive as the bloodthirstiness to which we have already referred.

It is necessary first to understand that some of the passages in question are, as scholars tell us, formal declarations of ritual purity, as for example Ps. 26:

> **Be thou my judge, O Lord, for I have walked innocently: my trust hath been also in the Lord, therefore I shall not fall.** (Ps. 26.1)

It is not necessary to ascribe unseemly vanity to the author of such verses, any more than to a defendant pleading 'not guilty' in a modern law court, or to think that when he swears to speak the truth, the whole truth, and nothing but the truth in that setting, he is claiming unfailing veracity on all occasions. We may compare the protestations of innocence in the early chapters of Job, a character whom it would be absurd to accuse of complacency. Yet when all this is said, the self-assurance of some of the Psalmists strikes us as being far from the confession of sins with which Christians are taught to open their acts of worship – and for which, indeed, they find material in other Psalms of a different temper from those mentioned, *e.g.*

> **Have mercy upon me, O God, after thy great goodness: according to the multitude of thy mercies do away mine offences.** (Ps. 51.1)

This sense of deep unworthiness in approaching God in his majesty and holiness is altogether in accordance with the finest Old Testament perceptions. The difference lies rather in the assurance of material reward for the faithful servant of God which runs all through the Old Testament, but (after Job's radical challenge) is turned upside down in the New. This expectation of prosperity and victory over adversaries receives its most systematic expression in the book of Deuteronomy – which, we may remark, is the one most quoted, after the Psalms, by Jesus in the Gospels. And indeed, human nature being what it is, the same view of religion has not ceased to flourish even after two thousand years of Christianity. It is still widely thought that the faithful worshipper of God should receive his reward in kind, together with the right to condemn the ungodly. Given our human nature, it is a creed much more likely to win popularity than the invitation of Jesus to his disciples to take up their cross and follow him, and his promise that in the world they would have tribulation.

We cannot say, therefore, that there is any 'solution' to this objection to the Psalms; but as in the previous case, we may think it wisdom simply to accept them as they stand, as a true mirror of human character. For we are no less prone to self-righteousness than those writers, though we may be more sophisticated about concealing it. Our public life, national and international, is riddled with it, as with an insidious disease; and it is, of course, the constant temptation of the Church, despite her calling to be the company of forgiven and forgiving sinners. Would the Psalms, then, be as authentic as they are without this frequent note of self-assertion – any more than the Gospels could speak as truly to our human condition, if they did not tell of the conflicts of Jesus with the righteousness of the Scribes and Pharisees? Many of these passages are unfair, we are often told nowadays by Biblical scholars who want to restore some credit to the Church leaders of the time. They are no doubt right, but the spiritual point remains more important than the particular historical one. It is the age-old desire of man to justify himself, usually at the expense of others, which stands defiant in us against the Cross. St Paul is the great exponent of that contrast which had marked his own life –

But God forbid that I should glory, save in the cross of our Lord Jesus Christ, by whom the world is crucified unto me and I unto the world. (Gal. 6.14)

We may be sure that, as a learned Jew, he was steeped in the Psalms, both those which breathed a confidence in the moral superiority of the writer and those which acknow ledged their utter unworthiness in the sight of God.

* * *

The two objections we have mentioned so far are both of a moral character; the third is of another nature and may be termed intellectual. It is simply this: can we, living so long after the Psalmists and inhabiting an altogether different thought-world, post-Christian and post-scientific, really make their words our own? Of course this objection could be urged against any great writings of the past, Shakespeare and Dante as well as the Bible, and the answer will always depend upon that timeless element of genius which belongs only to a small part of the literature of the world. Nevertheless, it is worth examining the objection a little more closely in its application to the Psalms.

In general terms, one of the greatest differences between us is that the Psalmists have hardly any belief or interest in secondary causes. In their view, the initiative, for good or ill, lies always with God, and everything may be ascribed to his agency unless it is due to the friends or enemies of the writer – and even then, they are often seen as the instruments of God's love or anger as the case may be. It is vain to pretend that most people's minds work in such a way today; though whether it is an improvement to ascribe the control of our lives to unknown people ('them') and impersonal forces is highly debatable. At any rate the concentration of the Psalms upon the relationship with God, not at the periphery but at the centre of human existence, is unfamiliar and perhaps for that reason all the more striking. Thus our knowledge of creation, both in its immensities and its details, is vastly greater than those of the ancient poets (and consequently, it may be added, our matter for praise and thanksgiving). Yet when it comes to the framework of this knowledge we might be hard put to it to improve on the Psalmists.

> **The heavens declare the glory of God, and the firmament sheweth his handiwork. One day telleth another, and one night certifieth another. There is neither speech nor language, but their voices are heard among them.** (Ps. 19.1–3)

Such a combination of cosmic vision and personal response is characteristic of the Hebrew spirit, and we find it again in Jesus and in Paul. It is a combination which may still speak to a generation which is grappling both with the wonders of the universe and with the depths of the human psyche.

It remains, however, for the modern Christian to ask if the Church should devote so much time and attention to the Psalms, given that they are pre-Christian and therefore inevitably sub-Christian to a certain extent. I think that we all now applaud those brave spirits of the 18th and early 19th centuries who decided that they must write Christian hymns and introduce them into public worship, even at the risk of being accused of importing unbiblical material. Many of these hymns, especially those of Isaac Watts, John and Charles Wesley, John Newton and William Cowper, have since become as much a part of the treasury of Christian devotion as the Psalms themselves. We should not wish, even if we were able, to return to 'David' alone or to be without our native songs of praise which have so often taken their inspiration from the Bible. (I am speaking here of Protestantism. The Catholic Church already possessed a great treasure in the Latin hymns of the middle ages).

And yet the Psalms have not been superseded, and we may surely affirm that this is not due to mere conservatism on the part of the Church. For they continue to speak for human beings who in spite of all intellectual and material advances – perhaps even in spite of a lifetime of faithful religious observance – find themselves vulnerable after all. Again and again we are 'brought up short' by the changes and chances of our mortal life: by the sudden loss of a job that seemed secure, by the collapse of a marriage, by the death of a beloved child, by the news that we ourselves have only a matter of months to live.

> **And in my prosperity I said, I shall never be removed: thou, Lord, of thy goodness hast made my hill so strong. Thou didst turn thy face from me, and I was troubled. Then cried I unto thee, O Lord, and gat me to my Lord right humbly.** (Ps. 30.6–8)

Such words pass no judgement on our weakness; they comfort us in the deepest places. So we may ask: what person who regularly reads the Psalms does not feel the warmth of their humanity, both in trust towards the living God and in the knowledge of our own extreme frailty of body, mind and spirit?

> **Nevertheless I am always by thee: for thou hast holden me by my right hand. Thou shalt guide me with thy counsel: and after that receive me with glory. Whom have I in heaven but thee? And there is none upon earth that I desire in comparison of thee. My flesh and my heart faileth: but God is the strength of my heart and my portion for ever.**
> (Ps. 73.22–25)

If I could say those words when my time came to die, I should not want many others.

Must we not conclude, then, by saying that the Church has done well to preserve the study and recitation of the Psalter, even though there are things in it which anyone who lives 'in A.D.' may dislike or even refuse to say? It would save a good deal of harmful misunderstanding if the Church were to repudiate a fundamentalist interpretation of the Old Testament and say, boldly and clearly, that Jesus Christ not only fulfils the Law and the Prophets but corrects or negates some of the elements to be found in the Psalms and other Old Testament Scriptures. Those who would be his disciples cannot merely baptise the Psalms by saying the Gloria after each one; they must read them always in the light of his own life, death and resurrection. Yet we remember also that for Jesus himself and his apostles the Psalms were the hymn book of Israel, among the foundation documents of their faith. In them we have a living link with what we know of his devotion and that of the early Church. Therefore we may continue to receive and use not only those few favourites which may appeal to modern taste – a taste notorious for taking the jam and leaving the powder – but the Psalter in its entirety. For so much of human life is there; but it is human life still awaiting redemption from him who came to be its Saviour.

4
What is Man?

Our consideration of the Psalms began with their sense of the majesty and glory of God, and the praise which these called forth from all his creatures. We go on now to think about the Psalmists' estimate of man. What kind of view of human nature is it that emerges from these poems?

After many years, I have recently been re-reading some of Homer's *Odyssey* to which a good many of my days at school and university were devoted. It is interesting to compare and contrast that mighty epic with the Psalms. Here are two pieces of literature from the very foundations of our civilization, each anything up to three thousand years old and still able to speak powerfully to us – and what poles apart they are in their views of gods and men, and the relation between the two! It is true that in both there is a great deal of coming and going between heaven and earth, and a constant amount of supernatural intervention in human affairs. But that is where the resemblance ends. In Homer, as has often been pointed out, the human beings – some of them, at least – are more noble and moral than the gods above. Too often on Olympus there is a kind of heartless frivolity, or even a jealous vindictiveness, which destroys our respect for those immortal beings. No wonder a seriously religious man like Plato thought that the young should not be allowed to read Homer. Rather is it the changes and chances of human life that move us in his poetry. For the tragic element there, as in classical poetry generally, is that man who is in many ways such a beautiful creature – handsome, brave, skilful, capable of love, friendship and loyalty – is doomed to so short a life and to a certain death. *Sunt lacrimae rerum*: there are tears hidden in the very stuff of life. If it were still fashionable to read the classics, our contemporaries might recognise a good deal that is familiar to our own age. We find in both the pride of humanism and the joy of prowess in various fields, all accompanied by the apparent indifference of whatever powers there may be in the universe. We do not easily escape from that haunting sense of transience and eventual futility which clouds our eager attempts to eat, drink and be merry.

The starting-point of the Psalms in some ways looks similar, but in reality is quite different. The writers have, on the whole, a low estimate of human nature. They are as conscious as the Greeks of the brevity and fragility of our life, and their sense of our mortality finds frequent expression.

> **Thou turnest man to destruction: again thou sayest, Come again, ye children of men. For a thousand years in thy sight are but as yesterday, seeing that is past as a watch in the night. As soon as thou scatterest them, they are even as a sleep: and fade away suddenly like the grass.** (Ps. 90.3–5)

> **But no man may deliver his brother, nor make agreement unto God for him. For it cost more to redeem their souls, so that he must let that alone for ever.** (Ps. 49.7–8)

The difference begins when the Psalmists consider what may be called the moral quality of man; for of this too they seldom entertain a high opinion.

> **As for the children of men, they are but vanity: the children of men are deceitful upon the weights, they are altogether lighter than vanity itself.** (Ps. 62.9)

There is no use therefore in expecting from such an unsubstantial creature the kind of heroic qualities that the Greeks admired. Nor is this just a case of distinguishing the virtuous from the wicked (which is commonplace throughout the Psalms). For the Psalmists show their awareness that most human virtue, or at least the virtue which other human beings recognise and praise, is deeply flawed. In particular, the wise man will be unimpressed by the appearances of human grandeur:

> **O put not your trust in princes, nor in any child of man, for there is no help in them. For when the breath of man goeth forth, he shall turn again to his earth, and then all his thoughts perish.**
>
> (Ps. 146.2–3)

> **For man walketh in a vain shadow and disquieteth himself in vain: he heapeth up riches and cannot tell who shall gather them. And now, Lord, what is my hope? Truly my hope is even in thee.** (Ps. 39:7–8)

Such a *memento mori* passed into the Christian tradition and was once a powerful element of it; but it has now all but disappeared under the twin influences of greater longevity and material enjoyment. Yet what wonderfully suitable texts Psalm 39 could provide for Parliament, the City, the media – and no doubt for the Church Commissioners as well!

We may be tempted to conclude, then, that the Psalmists are wholly pessimistic about humanity; yet that is certainly far from the truth. Quite a different picture is presented to us by Psalm 8 in particular, that marvellous little poem about man as the viceroy of creation – the Psalm which the author of the Letter to the Hebrews takes and interprets with reference to Jesus Christ (Heb. 2.6–9). The Psalmist's starting-point is, once again, the insignificance of the creature beside his Creator:

What is man that thou art mindful of him, and the son of man that thou visitest him?

When you look at the night sky even without the benefit of a telescope or modern astronomical knowledge, this little animal does not seem to amount to much. And yet, amazingly –

Thou madest him lower than the angels to crown him with glory and worship. Thou makest him to have dominion of the works of thy hands: thou hast put all things in subjection under his feet.

(Ps. 8.4–6)

Thus memorably is the theme of the creation story in Genesis taken up, that the beasts were brought to Adam to see what he would call them (Gen. 2.19), and that even in his fallen state he has not ceased, with Eve his wife, to be made in the image of God.

No other Psalm is quite as explicit as this one about the glory of humanity, but it would be a mistake to regard it as an isolated example. The 'praising Psalms', 145–150, with which the book ends so triumphantly, express again some of man's capacity for the good life in tune with God and the rest of creation. No one reading such words could reasonably maintain that the effect of the Psalter is to devalue our species or to degrade and depress human beings. The essential difference, however, from Homer (and from many people in our own generation) is that the Psalmists do not believe the glory of man to be *intrinsic*. They find it altogether in his relation to the God who made him and constantly watches over him. This relation begins with a sense of total dependence on his part, and the frequent attempts of human beings to deny this dependence or to pretend that it can be ignored are a folly that can only lead to a bad end.

> **Take heed, ye unwise among the people: O ye fools, when will you understand? He that planted the ear, shall he not hear? Or he that made the eye, shall he not see? Or he that nurtureth the heathen** (all nations, be it noted, not Israel alone), **it is he that teacheth man knowledge, shall not he punish?**
> **(Ps. 94.8–10)**

The opposite of such practical atheism is that relationship of complete trust between God and man which is the ideal of the Psalmists, involving us in a conscious reliance on the loving wisdom of our Maker. It is through such trust, and only through it, that man is able to fulfil his God-given vocation which is to be his viceroy and agent in the created order.

We may turn aside for a moment to think about that other great Hebrew poem which stands next to the Psalter in our Bible, *viz.* the Book of Job. Once again, the contrast with the Greeks is stark. There is a touching pathos in the *Odyssey* concerning the old man Laertes and the faithful dog Argus, but one could not easily imagine Homer choosing as his hero a man covered with boils, sitting on a dunghill and scratching himself with a piece of pot! Job is in the extremity of wretchedness – yet even in that condition he is always aware that what matters is his account with God. It is no use expecting to get an answer to such suffering out of the three comforters, Eliphaz, Bildad and Zophar, though they are no doubt doing their best (as so many 'comforters' have done since), poor irritating fellows plugging the orthodox line. The Book of Job is described as a drama about the suffering of the innocent, and so it is; but it is not at all the kind of drama characteristic of our own day, in which some martyred innocent is making a magnificent protest against a powerful oppressor and deifying the revolution. Job refuses to curse

God and die, nor does he lapse into atheism. His greatness lies in the trust which, through the intensity of his suffering, he retains in his God.

> **Thou wouldst summon me, and I would answer thee; thou wouldst have a desire to the work of thy hands.** (Job 14.15)

The agony of the sufferer is not just that he feels he is being very unfairly treated after leading such a blameless life. That claim is made, of course; but Job goes beyond it to probe the righteousness of God himself – his very reputation, we might say. Is the destiny for which he, the child of God and his intimate friend, had been created now altogether denied and frustrated? In that insistent question (which, as many critics have pointed out, receives no real answer in the *son et lumière* of chapters 38–41), Job proclaims his kinship with some of the Psalmists and prepares the way for the experience of Jesus in his death and resurrection.

* * *

The view of man in the Psalms which has been described is, in one respect at least, congenial to the modern reader. For it is a *democratic* one, *i.e.* within the compass of the most ordinary and under-privileged person. This is not surprising when we consider the Psalmists' frequent references to 'the poor', the losers in life's games. The Homeric view by contrast is generally aristocratic, though there are many kind words about faithful servants. It is pretty well unknown there for the gods to converse with, or come to the rescue of, servants or indeed women. Such an aristocratic view prevails in much of the great literature of the past, and makes a natural appeal to any class-ridden society (though its modern form should rather be called 'meritocratic', the view that if you are not in some respect successful, your opinion and experience are not of much account). The religion which emphasizes dependence upon God does not readily gain a hearing in such a society, and that no doubt is one reason why we do not often hear much nowadays (even in church) about grace, repentance and forgiveness. The season of Lent, for example, is easily comprehensible to our generation as an opportunity for brushing up our Christianity and our ecumenical fellowship, but much less so in its traditional teaching that –

> **The sacrifice of God is a troubled spirit: a broken and a contrite heart, O God, thou wilt not despise.** (Ps. 51.17)

In many of the Psalms, however, the writer is quite ready to cast aside what we, with our Anglo-Saxon temperament, would regard as decent self-respect and to acknowledge his utter dependence upon the loving patience of God.

> **As for me, I am poor and needy, but the Lord careth for me.** (Ps. 40.20)

It would be a mistake to regard such verses as mere admissions of material poverty or misfortune. They also contain what is much harder for the modern reader to swallow: *viz.* the confession of weakness, inadequacy, failure, sinfulness, on the part of the child of God.

> **So foolish was I and ignorant, even as it were a beast before thee. Nevertheless, I am always by thee, for thou hast holden me by my right hand.** (Ps. 73.20–21)

To those who believe that man has now 'come of age' (a phrase which seems less popular than it was fifteen or twenty years ago) and can stand on his own feet, the

Psalmist's words must seem as unpalatable as the Beatitude which says **'Blessed are the poor in spirit, for theirs is the Kingdom of heaven'** (Mt. 5.3). It is certainly being asked today if the Biblical view of human dependence upon God can still be sustained, or whether we ought not to regard it as belonging to the childhood of our race, or perhaps to the era when the Law was, in Paul's phrase, **'a schoolmaster to bring us to Christ'** (Gal. 3.24): a view, therefore, which can and must be discarded, as we survey the limitless possibilities of technology for our future. Christians can only reply that Jesus Christ seems to bear out the Psalmists in this matter. For the dependence of man upon God, of which they wrote, is expressed to the limit in the life which began, humbly and precariously, at Bethlehem and ended in the conflict between trust and suffering at Gethsemane and Calvary. Jesus lived as one who depended every hour both physically and spiritually upon his Father in heaven, refusing the normal props and insurances of a prudent human existence. His instructions to his disciples were of the same radical (and, as some would say, improvident) nature. He calls blessed those who are needy and know it, those who hunger and thirst after righteousness – and to the others who feel very little in the way of hunger and thirst he does not make much appeal. It is for this reason, and not because of some heavenly condescension of the *grand seigneur* variety, that the good news is proclaimed to the poor and that they are often the readiest to receive it. We have to look at Africa or India or South America today to see the most obvious examples.

Yet the good news is not (as the rich may hope, or scolding politicians deplore) simply encouragement to the poor to accept their lowly status – that could hardly be described as news at all! No, the news in the Psalms and in the Gospels is that there is no one so lowly that he is incapable of that relationship with God which is the real source of any human dignity worthy of the name. You are loved, you are accepted, the very hairs of your head are all numbered. As Jesus himself moved through a world that was frequently jealous and hostile, and according to the Evangelists constantly trying to trip him up and catch him out; as he pursued his way with a remarkable absence of fear and agitation; so he bids his people to put their trust where it rightly belongs, *i.e.* in their Father to whom they pray and who will not fail to hear their prayer. In such a way, by teaching and example, Jesus is the fulfiller of the deepest insights of the Psalms into the nature of man and the purpose for which he has been created. The dependence of humanity upon God is shown to be, not passivity, but an active dependence of love, for –

> **I have meat to eat that you know not of. . . my meat is to do the will of him that sent me and to finish his work.** (Jn. 4.32,34)

5

Out of the Deep

Some of the Psalmists' finest artistry lies in the way in which they move between the major and minor keys, often within the same Psalm. Hitherto we have thought mainly about the major; now it is time to turn to the minor, *i.e.* to those frequent passages which speak of suffering and oppression of various kinds.

> **Out of the deep have I called unto thee, O Lord: Lord, hear my voice; O let thine ears consider well the voice of my complaint. (Ps. 130.1–2)**

In Christian tradition, the Psalms called 'penitential' have been held to be seven, *viz.* Pss. 6, 32, 38, 51, 102, 130, 143, and these have been specially linked with the penitential seasons of Advent and Lent and other sober or mournful occasions. (The mediaeval churchmen, who liked such symmetry, named each of those Psalms as a specific remedy for one of the seven deadly sins.) We should add to these seven a further seven, which have become known as the Psalms of the Passion through their application to Jesus Christ: *viz.* Pss. 22, 23, 40, 54, 55, 69 and 88. In practice, there has been a good deal of overlap between the two groups, *e.g.* in our liturgical use in Holy Week. We may guess also that these Psalms entered into the mind of Jesus himself which would have been shaped by their devotion among others. To his people they have always spoken of his own *via dolorosa*, culminating in the cry of dereliction from the Cross. More widely, they may serve as a kind of anthology of worship in those times of grief, bereavement, loneliness, despondency and general God-forsakenness, which it is the lot of every normal human being to experience at some point in his or her life.

The reason why these Psalms have remained so close to the heart of our experience and our worship is surely the same as that for which the Cross and Passion of Jesus are to be found there also: both speak directly to the condition of human suffering, that condition which many other religions or philosophies have urged us either to ignore or to transcend, but which seems to persist universally through its many changing expressions. No doubt one would be guilty of a kind of temporal provincialism if one were to assert that the present century has a particular understanding of suffering; for humanity has always suffered, one way or another, and it may only be the scale of the age of two World Wars, of Auschwitz and Hiroshima, which makes us imagine that we are special. Perhaps, however, this immense volume of suffering in the modern world has been all the harder to bear because there was a time not so long before (as some of the optimistic hymns of the late 19th century bear witness) when it seems to have been thought that wrongdoing and needless pain were on the way out, and a golden age at hand. Well, we know better now – but those sensitivities which were sharpened by the hope of progress and by many material advances in our standard of living, help to make the suffering seem more acute than that which was borne by our much-enduring forefathers. The fact that we have lived among so many disappointed expectations probably explains our comparative absence of hope, which in the Psalms and in former days was often the anchor in the midst of tribulations. At any rate our Western and post-Christian society is conspicuous to the rest of the world for its lack of hope. There is an abundance of books, broadcasts, pictures, sculptures and musical compositions which faithfully and forcefully represent the dark side of human life without a great deal of illumination. To give, or ask for, 'a happy ending' is generally taken to be a sign of artistic childishness; rather, in order to avoid being hurt, one must take refuge in cynicism. It is worth while, therefore, to look again at the Psalms and to see how in their case suffering and hope – or should we say, trust – are constantly juxtaposed.

The first thing to note is their *uninhibited* character. Not for these Hebrew poets the classical restraint of the Greeks, the stoicism of the Romans, or the stiff upper lip of the British! If they felt terrible, they told the world they felt terrible – in the modern phrase 'they let it all hang out' – no less than with their emotions of joy, triumph and excitement. Again, it is a part of this uninhibited expression that they are so *physical* in their descriptions of what we might be tempted to call mental or spiritual suffering (as if the body were something apart, but of course it is nothing of the kind).

> **For my loins are filled with a sore disease, and there is no whole part in my body. I am feeble and sore smitten: I have roared for the very disquietness of my heart.** (Ps. 38.7–8)

Such physical torment, with its effects on mind and heart, finds its most famous expression in Psalm 22, the Psalm *par excellence* of Christ's Passion, where it gradually takes on the quality of a nightmare:

> **Many oxen are come about me: fat bulls of Bashan close me in on every side. They gape upon me with their mouths, as it were a ramping and a roaring lion. I am poured out like water, and all my bones are out of joint: my heart also in the midst of my body is even like melting wax. My strength is dried up like a**

potsherd and my tongue cleaveth to my jaws, and thou shalt bring me into the dust of death. (Ps. 22.12–15)

As before, we may lay such vivid verses alongside whole chapters of the Book of Job, and derive from the two an unrivalled vocabulary for the experiences of misery and suffering. When modern healers speak of the constant interaction of body and mind, and of the need for the whole person to be healed, they are speaking of a situation very familiar to the poets of ancient Israel. For the vocabulary of which we have spoken is not just of the 'where does it hurt?' variety. The Psalmists' perception of the unity of human personality is such that it is often difficult in their writings to disentangle bodily suffering from a consciousness of sin, a sense of guilt, and everything which separates the sufferer from God and other people.

There is no health in my flesh, because of thy displeasure; neither is there any rest in my bones, by reason of my sin. (Ps. 38.3)

For innumerable troubles are come about me; my sins have taken such hold upon me that I am not able to look up: yea, they are more in number than the hairs of my head, and my heart hath failed me. (Ps. 40.15)

How much conviction accompanies the recital of such words today? It was the simple belief of most Old Testament writers that all suffering is the effect of sin, either as a punishment for one's own offences or that of one's forefathers. That belief was unforgettably challenged, and as we should think rendered untenable, by the Book of Job. It received its death-blow from Jesus himself, not only from such words as appear in Lk. 13.1–5, but still more from his own redemptive life as the Suffering

Servant of God, foretold in Isaiah 53. It is, alas, true that the old belief about suffering as divine retribution is still held by many people in the modern world, Christians included, but it should have no place among those who have been signed with the Cross as the mark of victory. In a world where it is often the best, or the most innocent, who are apparently called upon to suffer most, the old equation simply cannot hold.

At the same time we ought not to dismiss too quickly the number of passages in the Psalms where physical suffering is aggravated, if not caused, by an acute consciousness either of personal sinfulness or by a general and confused sense of oppression by all that is wrong and evil. This is connected in the mind of the poet with the displeasure of God; for how could God, who looked at all that he had made and found it very good (Gen. 1.31), be expected to take pleasure in the wretchedness of his creatures? It is natural for the Psalmist to ask, therefore, if such abject misery is the effect of God's judgement and anger against him.

> **For when thou art angry, all our days are gone: we bring our years to an end, as it were a tale that is told. . . so teach us to number our days, that we may apply our hearts unto wisdom.** (Ps. 90.9,12)

This psychological insight of the Psalms is of the deepest, as even a nasty attack of 'flu can remind us, and it challenges all facile attitudes towards the tragic element in human life. There is nothing dignified in the moaning of self-pity, but despite all our brisk would-be comforters our sense of the tragic goes much further than that. It is **'the sin** (singular, not plural) **of the world'** of which St John the Evangelist speaks (Jn 1.29) and of which the Psalmists were so keenly aware, which produces the grief of our being. The common experience of bereavement brings this sense to the surface; for although there are some bereavements which are accompanied only by a radiant memory of faith and love, there are many others in which, as St Paul says in 1 Cor. 15.56, **'The sting of death is sin'**. That sting does not consist only in the sharpness of a sudden separation – rather is it the effect of separation from God and from one another, which may have lasted for years without being fully recognised or acknowledged. One aspect of the consequent suffering is *loneliness*, the sense of being utterly cut off from the company and comprehension of others. How well do the Psalmists know this, and how vividly do they express the truth that in general, people are not anxious to know about the sufferings of others! Or if they do want to know, it is only for a short time, after which they become bored and impatient with our grief ('it is time to pull yourself together'), and even if they love us and care greatly about us, with the best will in the world they cannot enter into our skin and share our feelings and experiences. Thus the hard truth is borne in upon us that even the best and most sociable of human beings must suffer and die alone.

> **I looked also upon my right hand, and saw there was no man that would know me. I had no place to flee unto, and no man cared for my soul.** (Ps. 142.5)

We find, therefore, in the Psalms that, quite apart from the many forms of sheer human wickedness – malice and cruelty – which appear there, frequent reference is made to human *inadequacy* when it comes to help in trouble or the assuaging of grief. And this corresponds to our experience in every generation; we should like to be able to comfort one another, but even the most compassionate soul is forced to recognise that, sooner or later, its resources must fail, and each one will bear his or her own burden unless God be there.

* * *

How may a Christian relate these reflections – and this theology – to the story of Jesus in the Gospels? We have already said that he utterly rejects the straight retributive theory of suffering as the judgement of God upon this or that individual. In no way does this imply that he underestimates the power of evil or tries to avoid it, in the modern manner, with careful euphemisms. Indeed, the whole story of his ministry can be seen as an unremitting struggle with that power – he does not go round suffering and death, he goes through them. For the Lamb who takes away the sin of the world could not do so without entering into the cloud, so that **'there was darkness over the whole land until the ninth hour'** (Mk. 15.33). So far from being unable, like one of the Greek immortals, to share in that hideous human experience in which are combined extreme physical suffering and the veil of sin which cuts us off from the face of God, he knew that condition to the uttermost. St Paul puts it in one of his daring flashes of inspiration:

> **He who knew no sin became sin for us, that we might become the righteousness of God in him. (2 Cor. 5.21)**

No less does the loneliness expressed by the Psalmists underlie the whole of the story of Jesus, from the temptations in the wilderness onwards. For although he is praised, followed and sought out by crowds of people, he is not understood and, indeed, (great communicator though he is) *cannot* be understood. His family love him after their own fashion and come wanting to see him – probably, as we should say, to take care of him. His disciples love him and want to do their best for him. Yet in both, Jesus can find a serious hindrance to his true calling.

The Synoptic Gospels, and especially St Mark, underline again and again what must later have seemed to the followers of Jesus their culpable slowness to understand and their failure at the critical time. **'They all forsook him and fled'.** The solitariness of their master in Gethsemane and on Calvary is only the culmination of what had been a solitariness consciously accepted ever since his baptism by John in the River Jordan. **'He saved others, himself he cannot save.'** Only to his Father could he look for sustaining power –

> **Nevertheless I am always by thee: for thou hast holden me by my right hand.** **(Ps. 73.22)**

We come back again to the God-directedness of the Psalms, but we come back to it not this time in the triumphal shout of confident praise, but in the faith that is holding on like (and in) grim death, in that 'nevertheless' which speaks so much. There may be times when we who live in an age of scepticism and sophistication feel that the religion of the Psalms is too easily won, and their professions of faith altogether too glib – 'if only it were as easy as that!' we mutter to ourselves. If all the Psalms had been of that kind, I think we should have abandoned them long ago. What links us with them, as it does with the Gospels, is the struggle of faith not only with outward adversity (though there is plenty of that to be found in both) but with the inward sense of loneliness and God-forsakenness, yes of an obedience which seems to go unheeded and unrewarded by the One to whom it is offered. It was Job who invented the phrase **'the skin of our teeth'** (19.20), and it is often by the skin of their teeth that the Psalmists cling on to their trust in God. Indeed, when we consider the whole story of the Jewish people, not least in this murderous century of ours, we may think that no phrase could be more appropriate to describe that history.

And in the midst of it we find Jesus the Jew uttering with his dying breaths the words of the Psalmists.

> **My God, my God, look upon me, why hast thou forsaken me: and art so far from my health and the words of my complaint? (Ps. 22.1, Mk. 15.34)**
>
> **Father, into thy hands I commend my spirit. (Ps. 31.6, Lk. 23.46)**

6

Who is the King of Glory

It is ironical to reflect nowadays that in the Age of Enlightenment two hundred years ago, kings were generally regarded as reactionary tyrants. To us who have lived into the era of presidents (whose little finger is often thicker than the royal loins), most kings have come to appear as benevolent and picturesque by comparison. And it has to be admitted even by enthusiasts for the Alternative Service Book that 'Rejoice, the Lord is president' would not sound quite the same. Yet both monarchists and republicans may take some comfort from the Psalms, as we shall see.

The words 'king' and 'kingdom' are very common in the Psalms. My concordance gives thirty references for the first and ten for the second, and this may not be an exhaustive list. A number of these references are to the pagan kings whose pride has been, or will be, shattered by the might of the Living God –

> **The Kings of the earth stand up and the rulers take counsel together, against the Lord and against his Anointed. . . yet have I set my King upon my holy hill of Sion.** (Ps. 2.2,6)

It is a common theme in the Old Testament that the arrogance of earthly potentates is to be rebuked, sooner or later, by the (to them) unexpected intervention of the King of the whole earth. This prophecy is fulfilled, for Christians, in the Kingship of the One who was **'despised and rejected of men'** – whose royal claim not even Israel was ready to recognize.

Nor is it only foreign rulers who come in for divine condemnation and chastisement. We may remember that throughout the Old Testament the writers are decidedly ambivalent about kingship in Israel and Judah. According to the Books of the Chronicles, about two-thirds of the monarchs were bad to one-third good, and the monarchy itself came to an inglorious end in defeat and exile. It is consistent with this history that princes do not get a good press in the Psalms, being called both tyrannical and unreliable (See Pss. 118.9, 119.161 *etc.*). So many are the references to the abuse of power and the oppression of the poor that we may gather a strongly unfavourable impression of what the monarchy too often became in the experience of the Jews.

Yet for all this the poetic figure of the King remains unsullied by such evil reputation. For this there is a simple reason: he is either David, or of the house and lineage of David to whom God has given his firm promise – or else he is the Lord Yahweh himself. Scholars have distinguished for us those Psalms which were written for a coronation or some other ceremony, such as Ps. 45 which is clearly an ode for a royal wedding, and on the other hand those which celebrate the divine Kingship and which begin **'The Lord is King'** or with similar words (Pss. 93–99 in particular). Yet in this matter the line between human and divine is not always so clearly drawn. To us this may appear strange, but in many cultures the King has been a quasi-godlike figure, and it is only some 300 years since our people ceased to believe in the divine right of kings. Thus we find some Psalms in which, although the King is evidently meant to be human, his reign is endowed with attributes which may almost be called divine. Pss. 21 and 72 come to mind, and above all the two Psalms often quoted in the New Testament, Pss. 2 and 110.

I will preach the Law whereof the Lord hath said unto me: Thou art my Son, this day have I begotten thee. (Ps. 2.7)

The Lord said unto my Lord, Sit thou on my right hand until I make thine enemies thy footstool. (Ps. 110.1)

To the early Christians these were the messianic Psalms, whatever they may have meant to the original writers. They saw them as prophetic of that unexpected Son of David whose reign was to appear so different from the exhibitions of power which the world associated with kingship.

All kingship, therefore, like all fatherhood, is seen to derive from God above. For in the Old Testament generally God himself is the King of his people, just as he is declared to be 'above all gods' and Creator of all things. We may remember his displeasure voiced in the Book of Samuel (I Samuel 12), when the Israelites first ask for a king such as the other nations have and receive the tragic figure of Saul. For Israel is not just like any other nation, it is a theocracy. Kingship is not to be guaranteed by mere heredity but by the gift and grace of God himself. Thus, although in the Psalms David and his heirs have received a divine promise which in the end is irreversible, they are still liable to error, failure and correction.

His seed also will I make to endure for ever, and his throne as the days of heaven. But if his children forsake my law and walk not in my judgements. . . I will visit their offences with the rod and their sin with scourges. (Ps. 89.30–32)

For the Kingdom of God is not expressed simply in conquest, much less in pomp and circumstance. It is to be found above all in justice and truth, mercy and loving-kindness, and the only ruler capable of such kingship is the one who is inspired and guided by God himself. Thus the Psalmist sings:

> **Give the King thy judgements, O God, and thy righteousness unto the King's son. Then he shall judge thy people according unto right and defend the poor.** (Ps. 72.1–2)

We who have grown so accustomed to the language of the Psalms and the tremendous claims which they contain may well have difficulty in plumbing their original audacity. For the national kingship of which they speak (idealised in the person of David and Solomon) was hardly one of imperial splendour. In a world of Great Powers – successively Assyria, Egypt, Babylon, Persia, Greece and Rome – Israel and Judah were tiny, insignificant tribes, mere shuttlecocks in the international game. We could as well imagine Poland claiming supremacy over the superpowers of our own day. Much of the vision of the King and his Kingdom in the Psalms, therefore, can only be taken as referring to a time to come, a time such as many of the Hebrew prophets had painted in thrilling colours. That promised time would be altogether different from the normal oriental one of autocratic rule, bribery, flattery, corruption and discrimination. It would mark the inauguration of a reign in accordance with the will of God and one that manifested his righteousness, to the joy of the whole world and its inhabitants.

> **Let the heavens rejoice and let the earth be glad; let the sea make a noise and all that therein is. . . for he comes, he comes to judge the earth; and with righteousness to judge the world and the people with his truth.** (Ps. 96.11,13)

To read such words in the actual context of Israel's history seems so wildly improbable that it is no wonder that scholars have dubbed them 'eschatological', *i.e.* referring to that end of history which we describe as 'kingdom come'. (And we may have a fellow-feeling with the Psalmists, for are not such words still eschatological today?) Yet the conviction that God is both judge and deliverer is never, in the Psalms, removed from the sphere of human affairs into a world of fantasy. It behoves us, therefore, to look more closely at that conviction as it speaks to Christians of our own day.

* * *

Power is not a popular word in Church circles nowadays. We have seen such ugly abuses of power in the present century and feel so threatened by its possible abuse in the future that there is no wonder we are anxious to dissociate ourselves from it – and the fact is that the Churches of Europe, both East and West, possess less power in their various countries today than they have done for centuries. It is no coincidence, therefore, (if the remark is not too cynical) that they prefer to talk about 'powerlessness' and 'standing alongside the poor', even if they do not have many poor among their members. No figure is less well thought of among us nowadays than the Emperor Constantine, who is held responsible for the confusion of Church with State and the inauguration of the 'Christendom idea' (though any fair-minded person would have to admit that human society would probably have been a good deal worse off without that idea). It follows, also, that the prayer for those in authority, even when like our own Queen they are known to be practising Christians, is usually more dutiful than enthusiastic nowadays. As the Church passes more and more into the status of a minority, and institution gives way more and more to movement, it is natural – though it provokes a good deal of indignation among governing parties in the State – that we should identify ourselves more easily with protest and dissent than with the kind of authority in society that was presupposed in the Book of Common Prayer. Modern liturgies are not usually thought of as political documents, but they have their political and social aspects also.

How should we view these developments in the light of the Psalms and, later, of the Gospels? In the world of the Bible, power is seen as a fact of life, and if it is not exercised well, it will be exercised badly. The figures of Pharaoh, of Ahab and Jezebel, and of Nebuchadnezzar epitomise this truth in the Old Testament, and those of Herod, Pilate, and the unnamed Caesars in the New. The misuse of power, in cruelty and injustice, springs inevitably from the arrogance of human beings who forget God or else decide to ignore him.

> **He hath said in his heart, God hath forgotten: he hideth away his face, and he will never see it. (Ps. 10.11)**

Such pretensions to absolute and unfettered power, however, are always a blasphemy, for they deny the dependence of every creature upon God and violate that kinship among all human beings, high or low, which God has ordained. Such blasphemy invites retribution, a judgement which will sooner or later fall upon it from the Divine Majesty. Sometimes the judgement seems to tarry long. The long-suffering of God with human oppression and wrongdoing provokes many a cry from the Psalmists, a cry which is re-echoed through the New Testament as far as the Book of Revelation in particular, where the saints call out 'How long, O Lord, how long?'. Yet in the days of darkness there is a fierce tenacity of trust in the King whose authority alone is righteous and in whose power it is to vindicate the right in the end.

> **For the poor shall not always be forgotten: the patient abiding of the meek shall not perish for ever.** (Ps. 9.18)

> **Arise, O God, and judge thou the earth: for thou shalt take all the nations to thine inheritance.** (Ps. 82.8)

The frequent references to the God of Israel as judge (*e.g.* in Pss. 7, 36, 50, 82, 96, 111, 143, 146) may be matched with those which refer to Him as merciful deliverer (*e.g.* in Pss. 3, 9, 18, 27, 33, 40, 64, 71, 76). It goes without saying that His judgement is neither arbitrary nor capricious, for the essence of His self-revelation to Moses is that He shows Himself both holy and unchanging, and in the Law calls His people to the same character.

> **No, I the Lord do not change, and you, sons of Jacob, are not ruined yet! Since the days of your ancestors you have evaded my statutes and not obeyed them. Return to me and I will return to you, says the Lord of Hosts.** (Mal. 3.6–7)

Yet simply to say that He is impartial, in the sense of a modern judge who is there to administer laws enacted by Parliament, would fail to do justice altogether to the moral passion which, according to the Psalmists and to Jesus, belongs to the Vindicator of right.

> **My song shall be of mercy and judgement: unto thee, O Lord, will I sing.** (Ps. 101.1)

It is a common feature of human thinking, and indeed of human religion, to separate out mercy and judgement, and for the sake of an imagined clarity to put them into separate compartments: *e.g.* the notion that a merciful Virgin Mary must intercede for sinners with her austere Son. The teaching of both the Psalms and the New

Testament about God is altogether more mysterious and profound. It proclaims that judgement and salvation are united in the same source – and are therefore declared by the same Messiah who is both Saviour and Judge of the world.

As we have seen, this Biblical unity has by no means always been preserved. There is a modern tendency to sentimentalise Jesus by turning him into no more than a kind of permanent 'leader of the opposition', no doubt in reaction to the ages in which he was displayed as the ally of government. Both pictures can only distort the fullness of the Gospels. For whether we take the parables of the Kingdom in the Synoptics or St John's presentation of the Son to whom the Father has committed all judgement upon earth, Jesus is certainly concerned with the authority of God. He will not accept for himself the title of King which both his friends and his enemies press upon him, much less a regal lifestyle. Yet he is quite uncompromising about loyalty to that King whom he has come to proclaim, and indeed about his own claims to represent Him.

> **Seek first the Kingdom of God and his righteousness, and all these things will be added to you. (Mt. 6.33)**

> **All authority in heaven and on earth has been given to me. Go therefore and make all nations my disciples. . . (Mt. 28.18–19)**

Yet this figure so confident in its majesty is the same Son of Man who is 'meek and lowly in heart' and who carries the sins and diseases of his suffering people. The marks of his kingship are love, healing, forgiveness and self-sacrifice. He reigns from the Tree. But in none of this is there any abatement of the sense of God's justice or of his awful purity – no coming to easy terms with Sadducee or

Herodian, with Caiaphas or Pilate. For again, as in the Psalms and the prophets, the idols of humanity are swept aside as vanity, and only the Living God is to be loved and served. All the time our eyes are directed to that end to which the whole creation moves, namely the consummation of God's Kingdom, and yet there is always a 'meanwhile'. It is here and now that the King is to be obeyed. **'Thy Kingdom come'** he taught his disciples to pray, **'Thy will be done on earth as it is in heaven.'** (Mt. 6.10).

In such a way we may trace the origins of the Jewish-Christian tradition concerning the relation of human power to divine authority, which (although often obscured) has done much to mitigate our natural brutality. Before the Israelites had kings, they had judges, even if many of the judges appear to have had swords in their hands rather than wigs on their heads. For the function of judgement was a key one to the people of the Law. One of the early pictures of Moses that we have is of him sitting to administer justice, and the same is true for Solomon. Throughout the Old Testament a ruler is himself judged by the way in which he has displayed the qualities of an upright judge, and especially by his evenhandedness with poor folk of no influence. This refusal 'to accept persons' is conspicuous, of course, in the ministry of Jesus; but we can already see in the Letter of James (2.1–9) that from the earliest times the Church has had a struggle to maintain that standard. Later Church history does not suggest that we have been particularly successful – yet the belief that a person, in or out of court, stands not just before human power but before those who are themselves accountable to God, has never perished from the earth. In our own day, we have had nightmares of its extinction in the novels of George Orwell and the actual behaviour of many a dictatorship. If we think that we can banish such nightmares by a simple appeal to 'human rights', we surely deceive ourselves; for since when have men, left to themselves, ever been ready to concede perfect rights to one another?

The Psalmists are not so naïve. They know that nothing less than 'the fear of the Lord', a genuine mixture of fear and reverence before the One to whom all mortals are accountable, will ever curb the natural desire of human beings to control and exploit one another. We have always to look away from our corrupted standards and practices to the source of a more perfect justice, for even if that justice will not be established before 'Kingdom come', the knowledge of it is deeply implanted in the hearts and minds of those whom God has created and redeemed. Is it not because this vision of the Psalmists at their best is so prophetic of Jesus Christ, and they in their own way often seem to be saying the same things, that Christians have continued so long to love the Psalms and make them their own? They are the hymnbook of a small and often persecuted people, and yet they speak for all humanity. Just so, the life of Jesus was brief and apparently tragic, yet it is endless. The Church, as Paul saw it, was politically and socially insignificant, yet it was the first fruits of the whole creation – 'ransomed, healed, restored, forgiven'. As long as time lasts, this paradox is shown to be true:

> **The foolishness of God is wiser than men, and the weakness of God is stronger than men.(1 Cor. 1.24)**

7

Captivity and Freedom

The theme of the foregoing chapters has been the way in which the Psalms, despite their great antiquity and initial strangeness, are able to speak to our condition today; and in particular, the way in which they are filtered, so to speak, through the coming of their fulfiller, Jesus Christ. If we may compare the Psalter to the light of an ordinary day, sometimes in sunshine and sometimes in cloud, the life of Jesus is like a great stained-glass window, perhaps the rose window of Chartres Cathedral. The light pours through that window and seems focussed by it. Yet it is also changed as it shines through into the church; new colours of rich beauty, deep reds and blues and greens, are cast on to the pillars and floors inside. There are, besides, dark patches and pieces of lead in the window which will not allow some of the light to come through. Even so, we may say, Jesus refuses to pass on some of those elements in the Psalms which we have noted, such as their occasional self-righteousness, their spirit of hatred and revenge. He affirms the deeply ethical character of the Holy One to whom the Psalmists had addressed their praises; he takes up every intimation of a Father who is 'closer than hands and feet' to his children on earth; and he is radical in his opposition to every person or impersonal force that would come between God and his people. But more than this, the pouring out of his life makes the words of that ancient poetry into flesh. **'A new commandment I give you, that you love one another.'** (Jn. 13.34). Thus T.S. Eliot's well-known lines from *Little Gidding* are verified once more –

And the end of all our exploring
Will be to arrive where we started
And know the place for the first time.

One of the consequences of this process of rediscovery is the Church's long-standing tradition of appointing 'proper Psalms' for the Christian festivals. Sometimes it looks as if a good deal of ingenuity had been needed, but more often the Psalm speaks directly to the occasion. Never is this more true than in our celebration of Easter.

I have set God always before me, for he is on my right hand, therefore I shall not fall. Wherefore my heart was glad, and my glory rejoiced: my flesh also shall rest in hope. For why? thou shalt not leave my soul in hell, neither shalt thou suffer thy Holy One to see corruption. Thou shalt show me the path of life; in thy presence is the fulness of joy: and at thy right hand there is pleasure for evermore. (Ps. 16.9–12)

In concluding these meditations, it seems a long way to descend from the hilltop of 'the fulness of joy' to the plain of our prosaic lives and their preoccupations. The appropriate Psalm for our situation is sometimes, by contrast, Ps. 137:

By the waters of Babylon we sat down and wept, when we remembered thee, O Sion. As for our harps, we hanged them up upon the trees that are therein.

And yet those half-remembered songs have everything to say to our present world, to its politics and economics, its social and family life. For the particular burden of our age is to be haunted by a sense of our own insignificance and meaninglessness, in a society where more and more seems to be done by the machines of our own devising, so that we are in danger of being reduced to the status of numbers. In the midst of such a society, it is the prime task of Christ's followers to help people to find a true sense of personal identity as the children of God and to foster communities of persons in our dehumanised cities – even sometimes our dehumanised countryside. In the carrying out of such a ministry the Psalms give us wonderful material for teaching and worship alike, for they combine the personal with the communal in an unforgettable way. As far as the personal is concerned, we have seen that the vocation of every man, woman or child on earth, whatever his or her degree, is to be addressed by the living God and to make a response. Just as this vocation is not confined to the rich or the powerful, neither is it confined to the highly educated or the professionally religious. It is not mediated by any kind of hierarchy. It simply belongs to the human being as such. What is more, it is not to be expressed only in terms of 'works', laboriously undertaken in obedience to a Divine Taskmaster. This latter may not be the explicit theology of our own age, yet with our committees and reports, our fund-raising and restless activities, we Christians of the West often give the impression that only by such meritorious service can we hope to glorify God; and in consequence the old and the very young, the unemployed and the handicapped, and indeed that large part of mankind which finds little time for specifically 'church activities', are all apt to be left on the sidelines as virtually useless. Not so the Psalmists, who are the prototypes of the poets and artists of Christendom. For they know that our calling always includes the use of our imagination; and however small our service to God may be (and it often turns out to be much smaller than our self-importance may have supposed), it is enough to justify our very existence that we have seen something of His glory in all His creatures and joined with them in the fulfilment of our being –

To live with Him and sing in endless morn of light.

Such imagination helps us to be at one with our fellows in a new way, for – as anyone who remembers choir practice can testify – it induces both humility and a sense of common purpose. Our solidarity with one another no longer depends upon race, class or any such thing, but only upon the vision which we share (and of which we all fall short), and it is a solidarity which ramifies into all our social relations, both at home and abroad. If we may take as an example our so-called acts of charity, the motto from the Psalms and the Gospels is –

As for me, I am poor and needy, but the Lord cares for me. (Ps. 40.20)

So often in the past church people, like others of their race or class, have concerned themselves with the poor and needy as with so many objects of benevolence. It is an attitude by no means easy to shake off in post-imperial Britain's dealings with the Third World, despite all our genuine feelings of compassion and desire to help. But the Lord *cares* for the poor and needy, directly and not just through our kindly offices; they are as much his people as we are, though we may find that hard to imagine! And it is that care of his, from cradle to grave, which gives them their true identity. For if this is indeed 'the century of the common man', in which millions of hitherto anonymous and powerless folk are struggling on to the stage of history, what are they going to find when they get there? Some ideologies tell them that simply by being there they will discover their true identity, but the evidence of our century is surely all against this. So much of the claptrap about 'the people' and their greatness has been used as a cover for cynical exploitation – so much of it conceals a terrible sense of disappointment and spiritual emptiness. It is the fact that their Father and Lord cares for them, calls them, speaks to them one by one, keeps company with them, and puts his Spirit within them, that alone gives them the meaning and dignity for which they were created.

Yet there is a further question to be asked. Have the Psalms anything to say to us concerning that perennial tension between authority and freedom, with which human beings have always lived and which takes many an acute form in our own age? 'The crisis of authority' is a commonplace of the pulpit today. It is widely assumed that all human authority, whether of government or of other institutions (home and school included) is of its very nature oppressive. Witness the almost automatic interest of the media in any who can be called rebels, dissidents or mavericks – never in those who conform or obey! At the same time, the world over, the burning question is 'how can we be free?', and 'freedom-fighters' (otherwise known as 'terrorists') spring up in country after country. The issue never appears simple. Those of us who are proud of living in what we call 'the free world' are nevertheless aware that that world lives in fear of nuclear warfare, of the fluctuation of international markets, of unemployment, of addiction to harmful drugs of many kinds and their consequences. An unkind observer might well ask us how it comes about that people who boast so much of their freedom have filled their squalid prisons as never before. Somewhere the mainspring of the relation between an authority which is feared but not respected and a precarious freedom has been broken. Our society lurches about from side to side like a bus that is extremely unsteady: on the one side, the danger of anarchy, of a permissive society going out of control, and of the retreat of many people into purely private judgement, so that all previously accepted standards of conduct, or indeed of truth, seem to have become slippery under our feet; and on the other side, perhaps in reaction to such anarchy or perhaps as its cause, the steady growth of state power, faceless bureaucracy, endless legalism, the inability of ordinary folk to get an answer or a decision from 'them', and the uglier threats of dictatorship with its suppression of freedom, its censorship of news, and its use of technology for its own sinister purposes. Even after 1984, George Orwell remains among the prophets.

In such a context we may look again at what the Psalms and the Gospels have to say about this tension. Their situation is certainly paradoxical. For the Psalmists lived under what we can only regard as severe constraints: the constraints of natural forces upon an ancient people, and a people, moreover, often subject to conquest and depredation by more powerful enemies. Not only so, but the modern liberal-humanist would add the constraints of a religion which seemed to bind the Hebrews with the constant fear of God's anger and punishment. It was no joke to be the chosen people of a jealous God! Yet despite all these unfavourable circumstances, we have seen how the prevailing attitude of the Psalmists to the divine authority which rules their lives is one of love and trust, and how often they speak of God both as Rock and Deliverer.

> **Whoso dwelleth under the defence of the most high shall abide under the shadow of the Almighty. I will say unto the Lord, Thou art my hope and my stronghold: my God, in him will I trust. (Ps. 91.1–2)**

> **I waited patiently for the Lord, and he inclined unto me and heard my calling. He brought me also out of the horrible pit, out of the mire and clay: and set my feet upon the rock and ordered my goings. And he hath put a new song in my mouth, even a thanksgiving unto our God. (Ps. 40.1–3)**

Unto thee lift I up mine eyes, O thou that dwellest in the heavens. Behold, even as the eyes of servants look unto the hand of their masters, and as the eyes of a maiden unto the hand of her mistress: even so our eyes wait upon the Lord our God until he have mercy upon us. (Ps. 123.1–2)

It is this conviction of spiritual freedom, under God's protection, which justifies the claim – a surprising one at first sight, in view of their history – of the Jews in their dialogue with Jesus:

We are Abraham's descendants; we have never been in slavery to any man. What do you mean by saying 'You will become free men?' (Jn. 8.33)

Such a claim, however, does not convince Jesus, for there is no religious guarantee, any more than a political one, of perfect freedom. Sin enslaves; routine, custom and convention enslave. Only the Son can make his friends free in his Father's household.

In the New Testament Scriptures, this paradox of the Psalmists is deepened. For the promised King, when he comes, appears as little free as the meanest of his subjects. Jesus is without power or influence, in the accepted senses of the world, even without home or income; at the beck and call of the ignorant and diseased, the incomprehension or betrayal of his followers; as a prisoner, a victim, an executed criminal, despised and rejected of men. It is a story which provides the very antithesis of our modern insistence upon our rights, for the Lord of all has deliberately divested himself of his supreme rights.

He did not think to snatch at equality with God, but made himself nothing, assuming the nature of a slave. (Phil. 2.6–7)

Yet this self-emptying is carried out precisely in order to establish the true rights of *every* creature and to bless human beings by restoring to them the dignity from which they had fallen. And it has continued ever since to be the calling of those who would follow Christ to surrender all rights and claims except that of joining him in his self-giving. People speak of the Sermon on the Mount as 'the simple teaching of Jesus', as if it were some code of commonsense which they could follow every day; but the truth is that it is a radical challenge to all our accepted notions of self-respect, self-defence, 'walking tall', and other familiar versions of Christianity. Only generous love, only the going of the extra mile, has ever made the world go round and continues to do so now. Such is the message that Jesus has brought us from his Father.

Of that message the Psalms give us only the foreshadowing, and yet they are already, to use the favourite word of our time, liberating. For they help to set us free from the tyranny of powers outside us and the tyranny of self within us, and confront us instead with the God of mercy and of judgement. They teach us to accept ourselves as we are, warts and all, and never to despair of God's love towards us. In a word, they are, as St Paul said of the Law, a schoolmaster to bring us to Christ, and a schoolmaster of a particularly lively and attractive kind. The reader will probably have observed that Psalm 119 is not among the favourites of this author – it is doubtless a sign of my immaturity that I have never outgrown impatience with that lengthy acrostic, full of rather smug reflections on God's statutes and ordinances! But I am ready to take the word of more mature Christians that this is a shallow view, and that the true value of that Psalm is summed up in the words of its 32nd verse:

> **I will run the way of thy commandments when thou hast set my heart at liberty.**

To have our hearts set at liberty: such is the universal human longing. To the Christian, the Psalms are prophetic of its fulfilment, for it was Jesus Christ who brought that freedom and released us from the yoke of trying to keep the commandments in an unliberated state. The Psalms themselves have ever since formed a part of our discipline in worship; but the discipline is never an end in itself, or it would be grievous. It is accepted in order that we may be released into our proper liberty, the company of him 'whose service is perfect freedom'.

Seven Canticles

Approaches

It has been the intention of this small book to consider that which sounds familiar but turns out to be strange, in various ways, to modern ears. It is natural, therefore, to take the Canticles in addition to the Psalms; for as long as Morning and Evening Prayer according to the Book of Common Prayer continue, these songs will form part of the staple diet of Anglican worship. This can cut both ways. On the one hand the words, which are often of great beauty, may become well-loved through their familiarity, and in an age when little is known by heart in church or in school, they may still nourish our spirits. On the other hand, the Canticles may run the risk of becoming hackneyed and stale through repetition. In many of our parish churches, however, Matins and Evensong have ceased to be well-known to the majority of the congregation, and it may well be that these are only acquainted with them through hearing them on the radio or in the occasional 'big service' in a Cathedral.

Meanwhile in choirs and places where they sing, the Canticles are wont to undergo that kind of shorthand which we may call 'Simpkins in G'. This means that they are well known professionally to that fairly small number of Christian worshippers who are musicians or choral singers; to the rest (who sit through them with delight or impatience, as the case may be) they are only set pieces for a performance which has little to do with their own devotions. In saying this, I do not mean to be either scornful or ungrateful – as a former chorister, I have delighted in many a setting, from Tudor times to the twentieth century composers. My point is that, even more than most of the Psalms, the Canticles are in danger of becoming so many 'heritage objects' in a liturgical museum, which can simply be produced, for example, to adorn a broadcast film with which they have no natural connection.

For the Christian worshipper, on the other hand, the question is 'What is their spiritual value for us today?', and it is with this question in mind that I have written. There is no attempt at a historical or critical commentary, only enough notes of this kind to provide the background. Since three of the Canticles are taken from the opening chapters of St Luke, *viz. Magnificat* (Lk. 1.46–55), *Benedictus Dominus* (Lk. 1.68–79) and *Nunc Dimittis* (Lk. 2.29–32), and we may add the beginning of *Gloria in Excelsis Deo* (Lk. 2.14) – recourse may be made, if desired, to the many commentaries on that Gospel. From the liturgical point of view, there is an excellent commentary, brief and clear, on all seven in *A Companion to the Alternative Service Book* by R.C.D. Jasper and Paul F. Bradshaw (pp. 105–130, SPCK, 1986). While acknowledging the good work that the A.S.B. has done on the Canticles, I have, as in the case of the Psalms, generally retained the Prayer Book wording and, with the exception of *Glory and Honour*, the old Latin names. This is done, not out of a defiant conservatism but simply out of the conviction that most Christians will still – though perhaps not for much longer – recognise the old names more easily or find them so printed in lists of cathedral or broadcast music.

I have not included those Canticles such as the *Venite* (Ps. 95) and the *Jubilate* (Ps. 100) which belong properly to the first half of this book. The seven chosen, being of very diverse origin, are a mixed bag chronologically speaking. The Lucan ones are clearly Jewish in style and akin to the Psalms, and yet are closely linked with the coming of Christ. All, however, have this in common: with the possible exception of *Glory and Honour* (but it may have been a hymn before it was incorporated into the Book of Revelation), each one has had a place in Christian worship since the days of the Early Church (4th–5th centuries A.D. in most cases). They therefore link us with many generations of Christian worshippers who have known them, often by heart, loved them and found in them meaning, solace, and inspiration. May the same be true for us still!

1
BENEDICITE, OMNIA OPERA

'O all ye works of the Lord, bless ye the Lord. . .'

The *Benedicite*, as it is colloquially known, is the only one of our chosen seven to come from the Old Testament, or rather from the Apocrypha. In our Bibles it appears under the latter as part of 'The Song of the Three Children' (vv. 35–65, N.E.B. Apocrypha pp. 202–3), whereas in Roman Catholic Bibles, such as the Jerusalem, which follow the Septuagint or Greek version, it is included in the Book of Daniel. In either case it forms part of the praise of God miraculously uttered by 'the three children' or young men – Ananias, Azarias and Misael, *alias* Shadrach, Meshach and Abednego – when they had been cast into the middle of a burning fiery furnace by the angry King Nebuchadnezzar of Babylon, as a punishment for their refusal to worship the golden idol he had set up. Consequently, this canticle is not only 'a song of creation', as the modern English title has it, it is also a song of praise uttered from the very depths of a cruel persecution. This, together with the exceptional refusal of these three successful young men to worship the golden idol, may give it a contemporary ring for 20th century readers.

What is the case *against* the *Benedicite* in our Christian worship today? First, that it is long, and secondly that it is repetitive. No doubt for this reason, the compilers of the A.S.B. have fallen in with the modern demand for brevity and have presented us with a much abbreviated version, passing immediately from the angels in v.3 to humanity in v.18 – and, of course, omitting 'Ananias, Azarias and Misael' whom they no doubt rightly assume to mean nothing to most of us. Very well! but, of course, this is to make something quite different from the original 'Song of Creation' which does not consist simply of sentient beings but takes in the whole of what we now call, with our characteristic elegance, 'the environment'. The Hebrews did not in the least mind being long and repetitive (the Benedicite itself only forms about half of the praises uttered in the burning fiery furnace), where the mercies of God were concerned. They thought they had plenty of time for those; they were enthusiastic rather than dutiful. Consequently when they thought about the works of God they tried to be as comprehensive as possible. It is not a small chamber group with which they were concerned, but an orchestra of Mahlerian proportions, in which every known instrument, high and low, great and small, is called into service.

Those who have no feeling for such an approach to the universe may sneer at the *Benedicite*, or regard its accustomed use by the Church in Lent as a suitable form of penance. Certainly I remember one otherwise intelligent writer saying he considered **'O ye ice and snow, bless ye the Lord'** to be one of the most ridiculous of petitions – you might as well go on "O ye bacon and eggs, bless ye the Lord" (and why not? Many a time do bacon and eggs seem a heaven-sent combination indeed). Perhaps such a critic had never stood in silence at daybreak looking at the Matterhorn. The majesty of mountains under ice and snow may seem to reduce a good deal of human pettiness to its proper dimensions of unimportance, but at least it serves to lift us up, as it did the Psalmist of old, to some small apprehension of the glory of the Creator. There is little enough about the creation in the liturgies of most of our churches – little enough to feed the obscure yearnings of those many people who claim to feel closer to God on the hillside or in the garden than in church. At least let us not lose what we have in the *Benedicite*, *viz.* the sense of humanity praising in tune with 'all creatures of our God and King', but rather build upon it.

Of course it may truly be said that the Benedicite is not a nature poem, in the modern sense of the word. It enumerates rather than expatiates. Its attention, as in the Psalms, is directed towards the Creator rather than to the details of his works. In this sense we may agree that it is archaic in its conception of the universe. How can any modern person with even a smattering of astronomy, physics or biology – it may be asked – remain satisfied with such a pre-Darwinian hymn? Our praise ought surely to be fed by a vastly greater knowledge of the workings of the world around us (as we see them portrayed, for example, in many beautiful and amazing television programmes about the lives of animals, birds, insects, plants and the denizens of the oceans) and by a consciousness of other worlds about us. In such a way, each generation should have its own *Benedicite* arising from its particular apprehension of nature as the sacrament of the Creator.

> And for all this, nature is never spent;
> There lives the dearest freshness deep down things:
> And though the last lights off the black West went
> Oh, morning at the brown brink eastward springs –
> Because the Holy Ghost over the bent
> World broods with warm breast and with ah! bright
> wings.

A hundred years after Gerard Manley Hopkins, in a world threatened with overpopulation, nuclear destruction, gross and greedy exploitation of all kinds of resources, we find ourselves in greater need of that 'dearest freshness' than ever before. The theme of the *Benedicite*, as of Hopkins' poetry, is that we need to seek it, not first in our own husbandry or manipulation of what we have been given – that must happen but it comes second – but in a passionate adoration of the glory of the Giver.

Finally, the song, however mighty, however universal in intention, must come down to the personal; for the greatness and beauty of the Creator and his works can only be seen through the eyes of each person, and no one else can make the response required of him or her. The author of the canticle knows that feeble though his voice may be, he *must* join in the chorus and not simply remain among the audience. Who then are invited to bless the Lord? Not, first, the great ones of the earth, not even the artistic geniuses, but 'the spirits and souls of the righteous' and 'holy and humble men of heart'; for it is they who can most easily forget themselves and their own small reputations and turn with simplicity and single-mindedness towards the centre of all things. Yet there is a further stage still. Although the writer himself may not be numbered among the righteous, the holy or the humble, he too has a contribution to make to the universal anthem which no one else can make for him. Do not, therefore, in the manner of well-meaning editors, excise the last verse, but for 'Ananias, Azarias and Misael' read 'James, Peter and Jeremy', 'Mary, Susan and Annabel', or whatever your name happens to be. For you, too, are a part of the chorus of the *Benedicite*, at one with the elements, the creatures, the generations of mankind: bidden together to bless the Lord, to praise and magnify him for ever.

2
MAGNIFICAT ANIMA MEA

'My soul doth magnify the Lord. . .'

Among the four Canticles found in the opening chapters of St Luke, the Song of Mary is the first – and it is right that the Lord's mother should have precedence. **'Young men and maidens, old men and children, praise the Name of the Lord'**, wrote the Psalmist (Ps. 148.12). So it is fitting that before the songs of the old men, Zacharias and Simeon – not to mention that of the angels who may be presumed to be ageless! – comes the clear, spontaneous, confident praise of a young girl (very likely in the Jewish tradition of early betrothal and marriage, what we should now call 'a teenager'). The song of Mary's joy has spoken to the hearts of all those generations who, in her own words, 'call her blessed', and perhaps most of all to her own sex, to her own age-group, and to those who were with child. If the history of Christendom, like the history of humanity generally, has often displayed the oppression and submission of women, it is good to observe that at the very beginning of the Gospel a woman sings of freedom and of a divine gift which no one can take away from her.

To go into the origin of these verses of St Luke is at once to be plunged into questions which, deeply interesting as they are in themselves, are of a kind to disturb those who have always taken the text at its face value. Why, for example, does the *Magnificat* occur in the context of Mary's visit to her cousin Elizabeth? Would it not come more naturally just after the Annunciation by the angel

Gabriel, or after the birth of the child Jesus? Is it possible that the song belonged originally to Elizabeth and was transferred by Luke to Mary? Again, how was the song known to the Evangelist? Was it – or were any of the subsequent Canticles – actually composed by Luke himself, or was it a part of the tradition of the Church, like one of today's well-known hymns, that had come down to him *verbatim*? Certainly it is not in any sense obviously Christian; the main point of the latter half is the identification of the handmaid of the Lord with 'his servant Israel', the nation that is now about to receive redemption and the fulfilment of God's promise. Yet the very fact that all these Canticles have such a strong Hebraic ring about them, so that Luke's infancy narratives sound like a little enclave of the Old Testament in the New, seems to argue strongly for their authentic and primitive character.

These are matters for scholarly debate, and in this book I have generally forsworn such enquiries and decided to take the Canticles at their face value, just as they have come to be used in the worship of the Church. One thing, however, is too plain to be ignored, and that is that the song of Mary reads like a New Testament version of the Song of Hannah in 1 Samuel 2.1–10, when after years of barrenness she becomes pregnant with her child Samuel (though the difference between the two songs should be noticed as well as the similarities). It is always apt to disappoint modern Christians when they first discover Old Testament precedents for what they thought original New Testament texts. Yet this reaction only shows that they have failed to realise from the outset how steeped in the history of their own people were Jesus and his apostles, and indeed the whole of that early Church which claimed (as St Paul expounds at length in the Letter to the Romans) to be the new Israel.

The theme of Mary's song is at once gloriously personal and also one which runs through the whole of the previous history of her people, finding expression in many of the Psalms and other books of the Old Testament: it is the power of God to turn the world upside down – to confound human pride and cause the last to be first. **'He hath put down the mighty from their seat and hath exalted the humble and meek. He hath filled the hungry with good things and the rich he hath sent empty away.'** We may refer these words to the story of Mary herself, a village girl from an obscure part of the Roman Empire called to be mother of the Saviour of the world, and chosen by God to be for all time the representative of humanity in glad response to his will: the Blessed Virgin, the God-bearer, Our Lady. We may also refer them to the whole story of Israel, a people numerically and geographically insignificant, frequently humiliated, oppressed, persecuted, and yet the chosen people of God and the instrument of his saving work for all nations. And it is in the approaching birth of the child Jesus that these two stories come together and melt into one – for as he was later to say of himself, he had come not to destroy but to fulfil.

Nor should we overlook the other side of the coin in Mary's celebration of the divine power, *viz.* that which concerns the proud, the mighty and the rich. Jesus was born into a world where those very qualities were being displayed and exalted to a degree hardly known before; and so little does the world change in this respect that two thousand years later, in the century of the dictators, the war-lords and the millionaires, they are still held in like honour. It was to be the Son of Mary who would show humanity another way and teach (as coming from the Source of all creation) another set of values altogether. He who was born in a stable and died on a cross, poor, homeless, unmarried, rejected, would challenge all earthly power and dignity, showing these for the usurpers that they are. Nevertheless it would be claimed for him by those who followed him in faith that he was **'Christ, the power of God and the wisdom of God'**. In that sense the song of Mary is prophetic of his whole ministry, not in Galilee and Judaea only but to the end of time. In our own day it is not easy for the affluent nations and churches of Europe and North America to escape those haunting words: **'and the rich he hath sent empty away'**. It is that emptiness at the heart of a Mammon-worshipping civilization which is the cause of so much of its sickness and its addiction to drugs of all kinds.

Christendom has quarrelled in times past over the Mother of the Lord, as it seems to do unfailingly over all the most precious gifts of God: the saints, the Scriptures, the Eucharist, the Holy Places. So skilful is the devil in knowing how to corrupt the best in our religion and turn it into the worst. In Mary's case we may be all the more thankful that we have the *Magnificat* and that it continues to be read and sung by Christians of varied allegiances the world over. For this triumphant song surely gives the lie at once to the sugary lady of much (dated) Catholic piety and to the neglected nonentity of Protestantism. The Mary of the *Magnificat* hardly appears as the prototype of female submission – or even as the clinching argument against the ordination of women to the priesthood! She did not accept that unique calling which God had conferred upon her with a kind of dull or fatalistic resignation; not so should we read the words **'be it unto me according to thy word'** (Lk. 1.38). No, she rose to meet her destiny with the strength which characterises her throughout the Gospel, and her response was one of a thrilling joyfulness. **'My soul doth magnify the Lord. . .'**: the English word 'soul' which might be taken as something disjoined from the body cannot do justice to the Hebrew word for which it stands.

It is with her whole being that Mary magnifies the Lord. And as we recall the sorrows that she would have to endure in later life – the sword which, according to old Simeon's prophecy, would one day pierce through that whole being of hers – we may be glad that the *Magnificat* remains her deathless signature tune: the 'yes to God' which only she could give and which she gave on behalf of us all, in all generations.

3
BENEDICTUS DOMINUS

'Blessed be the Lord God of Israel. . .'

'Blessed be the Lord God of Israel, for he hath visited and redeemed his people.' There could hardly be a more splendid opening, and St Luke has built up to it in dramatic fashion. First comes the announcement of the angel Gabriel to Zacharias and Elizabeth that (like Abraham and Sara, the very founders of the chosen people) they are to have a son in their old age, and the instruction that he is to be called John; then the incredulity and dumbness of Zacharias on hearing this tremendous news; then the joy of Elizabeth at the child's conception and her double joy at the visit of Mary carrying her own child Jesus; then the birth of Elizabeth's baby and his naming as John in the teeth of the surprise and disapproval of friends and relations (a good touch which never goes out of date!). Finally, as the climax of this story we hear of the end of Zacharias' dumbness; the Holy Spirit 'who spake by the prophets' comes upon him and he utters a song which like Mary's is partly one of rejoicing for his child and partly a rehearsal of the way in which God does not fail to vindicate and deliver his people Israel.

Again, the Biblical critics have come to cast doubt upon our traditional assumptions. In his commentary on St Luke (A. & C. Black, 1966), Professor Leaney is firmly of the opinion that the *Benedictus* is really a hymn of welcome to the Messiah and ought therefore to be taken as referring not to John the Baptist but to Jesus himself. Who then would be the singer of this hymn? Leaney mentions the suggestion that the singer is really the prophetess Anna in the Temple (Lk. 2.38). He points out that after an elaborate introduction to Anna, we are only told rather lamely that **'she spoke of him (the infant Jesus) to all those who were looking for the redemption of Jerusalem'**, and thinks that the Canticle belongs to her. This suggestion is attractive enough. It would make the *Benedictus* into the prophetic witness of an old woman instead of that of an old man – but why then should Luke, the least sexist of the New Testament authors, have transferred it to Zacharias, or at what stage in the early tradition of the Church could such a transference have been made?

Here is a riddle we are never likely to solve, and it is therefore my intention, as before, to take the canticle at its face value and to refer it to John the Baptist and his parents. This in itself is altogether welcome; for every one of the Gospels begins with the figure of the Forerunner and his witness to the imminent approach of the Christ whose shoe he is not worthy to unloose. Yet John himself is very far from being a minor character on any ordinary reckoning. Dedicated to God from his birth like the Nazirites of old, he becomes first a solitary hermit and then a powerful prophet and religious reformer. He is the fearless critic of kings and indeed of every rank of society, and this very fearlessness leads to his imprisonment and execution by Herod (Mt. 14.3–12). The New Testament itself, and modern scholars of it, make it plain that John's movement and his disciples continued well into the time of Jesus' earthly ministry, if not beyond. No wonder he is described by Jesus as the latterday Elijah whose return had been promised to Israel. The coming of Jesus to John for baptism – the turning point of the former's life and the moment at which his ministry begins – is one of the most moving episodes in the Gospels, as the Orthodox tradition has well understood in its beautiful ikons of that event.

In Christian understanding, therefore, John is both the last great figure of the old Israel and 'the prophet of the Highest', going before the Lord to make ready his ways. The contrast between the characters of the Forerunner and the King is memorably drawn in Mt. 11.16–19. The necessary work of rebuke and threat of divine judgement is the hallmark of John's preaching and it is clearly implied that, as in this canticle, there can be no real **'knowledge of salvation'** without **'forgiveness of sins'** – which was the aim of John's baptism. Yet it still remained for that forgiveness to appear fully embodied in a human life and for 'the tender mercy of our God' to be expressed in a way that could never be removed. All this could only be found in the one who was to come, the promised Messiah; and when he came, as the Evangelist says

> **we beheld his glory, the glory as of the only-begotten of the Father, full of grace and truth.** (Jn 1.14)

The Church's calendar gives John the Baptist's birthday as 24 June, Midsummer Day, and the day of his death by the executioner's sword as 29 August – but John's season above all is Advent, the time of eager expectation of the Lord's coming. To us he is the first of the saints who points away from himself to Christ as the fulfiller. In the vivid phrase which the Fourth Gospel ascribes to him (Jn. 3.29), he is the best man who stands beside the bridegroom, rejoicing to hear the bridegroom's voice and to know that it is he who has the bride. Therefore – **'he must increase, but I must decrease'.** And so it has been always in the history of our salvation, yet, for that very reason, John can never lose his place in that history. For that unselfishness which is his greatest badge of honour – which makes of him not just a hero but a saint – is the very type of our Christian calling. To everyone who loves and serves King

Jesus there is a self-effacement to be accomplished (as we saw first in the case of Mary his mother) in order that the King himself may increase – in order that he may carry out his saving work in his own way. It is in his Kingdom, as he himself promised, that those who have died to self will find their glorious fulfilment; for many who are first will be last and the last first.

'. . . whereby the dayspring from on high hath visited us.' We should be loath to lose that lovely poetic phrase, but some scholars have suggested that the original Greek word, here translated 'dayspring', refers not to a thing but to a person, a branch from the stock of Jesse, and thus the Messiah **'who has risen from on high'**. Even if this were right, it would not alter the general sense which is that of bringing light **'to them that sit in darkness and in the shadow of death'**. This Canticle, so full of echoes of the prophet Isaiah, recalls that other verse of his which Matthew uses of the beginning of Jesus' ministry in Galilee:

> **The people who sat in darkness saw great light, and to those who sat in the region and shadow of death light has sprung up.** **(Mt. 4,16)**

In the Middle East the dawn is a good deal less gradual and tentative than in our Northern climes, so we may say that the appearing of John the Baptist and his mission of repentance were indeed a 'dayspring' of some brilliance. Yet this was only the prelude to the time when the sun would be up in the sky, and all would be revealed at last. For that time, John did not have to wait long; when Jesus came to him by the bank of the Jordan it was already there. We are told that later on (and it is a mark of the humanity of John) in the darkness and loneliness of his imprisonment John was evidently seized with doubts and sent messengers to Jesus, asking **'Art thou he that should come,**

or do we look for another?' (Mk. 11.2). The reply of Jesus was thrilling: the promised Messiah had indeed come, and the mission had already begun, **'to give light to them that sit in darkness and in the shadow of death, and to guide our feet into the way of peace'**. Every time we hear or sing this Canticle we may think of them together, the two cousins, John and Jesus, the herald and the king, who lived and suffered alike for God's cause.

4
GLORIA IN EXCELSIS DEO

'Glory to God in the highest. . .'

Some Canticles have musical resonances beyond themselves. Thus the *Benedicite* may lead one into Haydn's *Creation*, that celebration of the beginning **'when the morning stars sang together and all the sons of God shouted for joy'** (Job 38.7). And to me at least, *Gloria in Excelsis Deo* always recalls what is perhaps the most sheerly joyous piece of Christian music known to me, Bach's *Christmas Oratorio*. When the angel's pure voice sings to the shepherd 'Fear not, for behold I bring you tidings of great joy which shall be to all people', Christmas comes again, whether one is a child or well up in years, and the world seems to be reborn.

This canticle links the New Testament Scripture with subsequent Christian history, embroidering the original message of the angels. For while its starting-point is in Luke 2.13–14, in its entirety it is a hymn emanating from the 4th Century A.D. with some variations in the early texts (see Jasper and Bradshaw, *A Companion to the A.S.B.* p. 113) – and being a hymn, we may add, it should always be sung standing up and not muttered upon the knees in the mistaken reverence of old-style Anglicanism! Two further things are of interest in the history of this hymn. First, that it began life as a Canticle in the Church's Morning Prayer – as it is in the East to this day and as one new option in the A.S.B. – and was only transferred to the Mass after two or three hundred years of usage; and secondly, that, in Rome at least, its use in the Mass was for a very long time confined to festivals, 'high days and holidays'. There is a relic of this restriction in the fact that Anglicans still do not use it in Advent and Lent, the penitential seasons; but perhaps we have become so familiar with it that we do not think of it sufficiently, in the manner of our Christian forefathers, as a song so beautiful as to be kept for special occasions.

'In earth peace, goodwill among men' has virtually become the motto of our modern Christmas, a motto certainly not to be despised in a world that is often extremely short of both. Yet it is almost certain that whatever the original Greek means, it does *not* mean 'goodwill among men'; Leaney (*op. cit.*, p. 96) renders it 'men of his favour'. Perhaps the modern version in the A.S.B. has done well to bypass the problem and simply say **'Glory to God in the highest and peace to his people on earth'.** Yet since we are concerned here not so much with textual accuracy as with spiritual meaning, we may surely hold on to the notion of God's favour towards humanity being reflected in our loving-kindness towards one another – for this part of the story of the Incarnation at least has not faded from the public consciousness. **'We love because he first loved us'** (1 John 4.19), and love came down at Christmas.

After this, the canticle takes the form of a doxology, or giving of glory, in three distinct acclamations (as can be seen in the Book of Common Prayer or more clearly in the A.S.B.). The first is addressed to God the Father and the second two to Jesus Christ, God the Son, with a mention of God the Holy Spirit near the end. It is a structure which recalls both the *Te Deum*, as we shall see later on, and the Creeds which belong to the same period of the Church's history. We are struck by something characteristic of that period, namely that theology and devotion are found together in harmonious marriage. It is the reproach of latter-day Christianity that theology should have come to seem to so many people dull, abstract, long-winded, prosaic, irrelevant (as the word 'theology' is used in the media today). These Canticles remain, however, with their clear and simple bone-structure to bear witness to the fact that the most passionate prayer of adoration can be united with a statement of belief. 'We give thanks to thee for thy great glory' – not, as nearly always, for this or that tangible benefit conferred on ourselves, but simply 'for thy great glory', for God's own majesty. 'For thou only art holy, thou only art the Lord, thou only, O Christ, with the Holy Ghost, art most high in the glory of God the Father.'

The idea that theology is, properly speaking, a form of doxology or giving glory to God (not to the reputation of the theologian!) has been gaining some ground recently in the West, probably as a result of our greater contact with the Orthodox Churches which have always held fast to this conjunction. We may say that it results from a realisation of two things: first, that the human mind is a precision instrument; but secondly, that God Himself is past our powers of expression, 'incomprehensible' in the strict sense of our being unable to grasp Him in his fulness. If the human mind is a precision instrument, that is how its Creator has intended it to be in any of the arts and sciences; and the fact that Anglo-Saxon people have had a tendency to sloppiness in their religious thinking merely shows that they do not rate religion highly, for they do not display the same kind of sloppiness in other disciplines, all the way from nuclear physics to sport. The Bible itself does not encourage us to worship any old thing in any old way. In both Old and New Testaments there is a constant process of refinement, a turning away from idolatry of all kinds to worship the Living God. Yet at one and the same time (and it is this which creates the tension in theology between an intellectual discipline and a form of worship) God is never to be captured and domesticated within our human categories of thought. He is 'above all that we ask or think', and all things – as at the death of our bodies – go off into mystery. If in our Western tradition, with its juridical bias and its tendency towards over-definition, we have lost this basic sense of mystery, *Gloria in Excelsis Deo* and the other Canticles are there to help to restore it to us.

It would be wrong, besides, to think of this Canticle as if it were merely a loud whoop of joy – as if that were the only way in which we glorified the Father and Giver of Jesus Christ. For the second stanza strikes quite a different note: 'O Lord God, Lamb of God. . .' at once recalls the sacrifice of the Cross and brings us close to that other 'communion song' of the Eucharist, known as *Agnus Dei*. It would falsify any properly Christian hymn of praise to speak only of the triumphant majesty of God and not also of the cost of our enmity towards Him – for such is the meaning of 'the sin of the world'. We may be grateful to the A.S.B. for having restored the singular here in place of the plural 'sins'. William Temple explained the point for us in his *Readings in St John's Gospel* (on Jn. 1.29, p. 24):

> It is not 'sins', as by a natural early corruption of the text men were led to suppose, but 'sin'. For there is only one sin, and it is characteristic of the whole world. It is the self-will which prefers my way to God's – which puts me in the centre where only God is in place. It pervades the universe. . . we are not 'responsible' for it; but it sets us at enmity against God; it is 'the sin of the world'.

Gloria in Excelsis, then, celebrates the Son as Saviour, and not only as a Saviour belonging to the past, but as one whose mercy and interceding power are implored for us too, here and now. The modern version puts this rather briskly, almost prosaically, but the rhythm of the Prayer Book version is repetitive like that of a mantra: 'Thou that takest away the sins of the world, have mercy upon us. . . thou that takest away the sins of the world, receive our prayer. Thou that sittest at the right hand of God the Father, have mercy upon us.'

Even a fairly insensitive listener to carols at Christmastide cannot but be struck by the clear and uncomplicated joyfulness of the carols which have come down to us from the Middle Ages. They have the spontaneity of childhood about them, and that is why they still speak to so many hearts. But when we examine their words, we find that their joy in Christ's coming is nearly always connected with the deliverance from sin, from punishment, from woe. They are so merry because they are songs of liberation – and it is the absence of that same sense of liberation from sin which causes the vapidity of so many modern 'Christmas celebrations'. The holly and the ivy are not just pretty decorations for the house –

> The holly bears a berry
> As red as any blood,
> And Mary bore sweet Jesus Christ
> To do poor sinners good.

It is not, heaven knows, that we live in an age which has outgrown the need of a saviour. Our society, you might say, is littered with failed messiahs – politicians, scientists, doctors, social workers, and so on – and in its disappointment with their unfulfilled promise society turns on these servants and rends them. In the world at large, no century could show a greater number of dictators than ours, who in their lifetime have received the adulation paid to gods, only to be cast on to the rubbish-heap of history within a matter of ten or twenty years after they have gone.

It has become one of the chief marks of authority in Church or State to bear the blame (whether at the time or posthumously, whether justly or unjustly) for the general wrongness of things. Christians whose faith is in the atonement of Jesus and his Cross will not be surprised at this age-old desire for a scapegoat – only sad at the failure to see where forgiveness and reconciliation to God have already taken place in **'the Lamb slain from the foundation of the world'** (Rev. 13.8).

The Christian hymns, therefore, from *Gloria in Excelsis* to the medieval carols are like the Psalms which went before them. They do not look for salvation to human efficacy of any kind; they do not expect to find it within the confines of space and time at all. It comes to them 'from the beyond' – and yet, astonishingly, the means by which it comes is found in weakness, suffering, even in seeming abandonment by God. Such is the mystery of the Incarnation, the mystery of Christ's glory; and it is to that glory that the whole of this Canticle points us.

5
NUNC DIMITTIS

'Lord, now lettest thou thy servant . .'

I remember once quizzing a class of choirboys about the Psalms, hoping (no doubt foolishly) to draw out some appreciation of that which they were singing in the Cathedral every day. 'Which is the best Psalm?' I asked. A hand shot up instantly: 'The 117th – it's the shortest!' The *Nunc Dimittis* is no doubt loved for other reasons than that it is the shortest of the traditional Canticles, but its brevity is certainly part of its beauty. It consists of one sentence, a serene hail and farewell. For seventeen centuries it has formed part of the evening worship of the Church. In the monastic tradition it belonged to the late night office of Compline, which has again become popular among many church people in modern times. In the Book of Common Prayer, Cranmer transferred it to Evensong. At whatever time, it seems to mark the perfect ending to a day – and in the same spirit it is often used as the closing hymn of a funeral service. But whenever it is sung, it is assuredly not meant to be dragged out as if it were a dirge set to the slowest of Anglican chants! For this is a canticle of gratitude, of confidence, and of peace, such that we may link it with the last words of Jesus himself from the Cross (Jn. 19.30, Lk. 23.46):

> **It is accomplished. . . Father, into thy hands I commend my spirit.**

Like Zacharias, the poet of the *Benedictus*, Simeon and Anna here represent in Luke's narrative the end of the old dispensation and the beginning of the new. In both cases the speakers are filled with the Holy Spirit, which means that what they utter is inspired after the manner of the Old Testament prophets. This canticle, short as it is, contains many echoes of the prophecies of Second Isaiah, especially 49.6 –

> **It is too light a thing that you should be my servant to raise up the tribes of Jacob and to restore the preserved of Israel. I will also give you for a light to the Gentiles, that you may be my salvation to the end of the earth.**

The difference between Zacharias and Simeon, however, is also worth noting. In the case of the former, the birth of his son John in his old age comes as an unexpected miracle and finds him naturally incredulous, and even anxious – for now he has to look to the future in his own family in a way altogether unforeseen. With Simeon it is different. We are told that he and Anna had been waiting **'for the consolation of Israel'** – a phrase that recalls the wonderful opening of Isaiah 40 ff – since they were assured that this would be revealed to them before their death. So these two faithful people had continued their long service in the Temple, but now the waiting was over and life held no more for them. 'Lord, now you let your servant go in peace: your word has been fulfilled. . .' The word *dimittis*, like so many biblical words, has more than one meaning and is full of resonance. Most plainly, it refers to the release of an old person in death; but it carries also the association of the freeing of a slave ('manumission', in the Roman term). For Simeon, death is not something to be feared, but rather to be welcomed as the consummation of God's promise; for he has lived to see that 'all shall be well, and all manner of thing shall be well'.

Apart from Christmas, Candlemas (on 2 February: otherwise known as the Presentation of Christ in the Temple, or the Purification of St Mary the Virgin) is one of the most popular of our festivals, and it is easy to see why. For this is as near a celebration of the whole family as we can find in the Gospel: Simeon and Anna acting, as it were, like honorary grandparents for Mary, Joseph and the child Jesus – age, youth and infancy linked in a single joy. Not only so, but this takes place in the Temple. Joseph and Mary who appear first in the Gospel as 'displaced persons' or refugees now return to the very heart of their own country and its religion and, poor as they are, make their thank-offering in accordance with the Law of Moses. It is the beginning of Jesus' acquaintance with the Temple, an acquaintance which runs like a thread through the whole of his earthly life. As a boy of twelve he is found there, sitting among the teachers of the Law and asking questions. As a man, he himself teaches there daily and the people flock to him. He drives out the money-changers in passionate anger against those who have turned **'the house of prayer for all nations'** into a den of thieves. He weeps over the coming destruction of that holy place, where not one stone will be left on another. Finally, at his trial he is accused of having spoken against the Temple and said that he would destroy it – and at the moment of his death the veil of the Temple is rent from top to bottom, and a new and living way, through his own sacrifice, is opened up to our Father in heaven.

In this whole story of Jesus and the Temple, an 'ambivalent' one, to use a favourite modern term, we can find a striking example of the joy and sorrow which are mingled in Simeon's prophecy to Mary: **'This child is destined for the fall and for the rising of many in Israel. . .'** Were some to rise and others to fall, as they either accepted or rejected Jesus as the Christ? Or were *all* destined to fall with his death and rise through his own rising again from the dead? **'Jesus said: Destroy this temple, and in three days I will raise it up. . . but he spoke of the temple of his body.'** (Jn. 2.19, 21). The prophecy of Simeon, like many of its kind, remains obscure but pregnant with meaning.

On the other hand, his last words to Mary are only too clear: Jesus is destined to be a sign to be rejected, and a sword would pierce through her own soul too, so that the secret thoughts of many would be laid bare. This little child, now God's gift and blessing to Mary and Joseph, would yet be the cause of much sorrow; and the vocation of all those closest to him, from Mary onwards through all the centuries, would be to bear a share in his sufferings. In one of his daring phrases (Col. 1.24), Paul says that he **'fills up in his body that which is lacking of the sufferings of Christ'**; and yet no one speaks more often of the joy of his ministry. That the two lie very close together has always been known to Christ's people, not least to those who, like Mary, have known the death of a child at an early age. This story tells us that such sufferings were to be neither fruitless nor meaningless, for within them lay the whole judgement of God, and His mercy too, on the hidden and often dissembling hearts of humanity. Jesus, as the revealer of the Father, walks in the light and brings to bear upon our human life the awesome light of that source from which he comes: namely, the One to whom we are wont to pray

> **Almighty God, to whom all hearts are open, all desires known, and from whom no secrets are hidden, cleanse the thoughts of our hearts, by the inspiration of your Holy Spirit that we may perfectly love you and worthily magnify your holy name; through Christ our Lord. Amen.**

6
GLORY AND HONOUR

'Glory and honour and power are yours by right. . .'

An English title forms the exception in the seven canticles I have chosen. The reason is that this one does not appear in the Prayer Book or in the traditional services of the Church in the West, but has come straight from the Bible into our modern service-books. The Church of Ireland (usually more adventurous in these matters) must claim the honour for its introduction, and now it finds a place in the A.S.B., p. 67, as one of the options for use at Evening Prayer. Together with another brief canticle, *Great and Wonderful* (A.S.B. p. 54), it is taken from the Book of the Revelation of St John the Divine, or Revelation (singular, *not* plural!), as it is usually called for short. *Glory and Honour* is a skilful conflation of three verses of that book, 4.11, 5.9 and 5.10, and occurs as one of the hymns heard by John in his vision of heaven and its worship.

Christians are apt to be sharply divided on the subject of the Book of Revelation, and this is no new thing either, for it was some centuries before it was admitted by the Early Church to the canon of Scripture. There have been, and there still are, those to whom it is *the* book of prophecy, revealing the destiny of creation and of mankind, and every detail of its strange imagery carries a message for those who possess the key to it. Such interpreters of the passages concerning the Antichrist, the Beast, the Scarlet Woman, the Millennium, and Armageddon have generally been regarded as cranks and fanatics – not least because they seldom agree among themselves – by

Christians of a quieter and more nervous disposition; and consequently a good deal of prejudice has been generated against the Book of Revelation itself. Most of this prejudice, however, could be dissipated by recourse to any good modern commentary on the book; for this would soon explain the category of apocalyptic literature to which Revelation (like the Book of Daniel and a number of other Jewish writings) belongs. Such literature generally arises at a time of severe pressure upon the faithful, and with cryptic references to present hardships and future deliverance seeks to comfort and strengthen them. Thus Revelation contains a great many coded references to the persecution of the Church by certain Roman Emperors and to her coming vindication and triumph at the coming of Christ.

It is more usual, however, to find within the membership of what are called 'the mainline Churches' those who have mixed feelings about Revelation. Some of its fantastic imagery they find repugnant and even nightmarish, yet there are many passages, particularly in the first and last sections of the book which seem to them as beautiful and powerful as anything in the New Testament, and which they would not lose from the Bible for anything: for example 3.20 **'Behold I stand at the door and knock. . .'**, or the vision of heart-lifting beauty at the beginning of chapter 21 where John sees **'the holy city, new Jerusalem, coming down from God out of heaven, prepared as a bride adorned for her husband.'** And whatever our general attitude to Revelation may be – and whether we find John's vision of heaven glorious or unappealing – we may appreciate the wisdom of taking these two short canticles from a book of Scripture very different from the other one which has been our source hitherto, *viz.* St Luke's Gospel.

The tone of Luke may generally be described as serene, and we know that as a Gentile he was anxious to commend faith in Christ to his fellow-Gentiles, and that he was therefore disposed to present the ruling power of Rome in as favourable a light as possible, without falsifying the story. Revelation comes out of a very different situation and is animated by a different spirit. Its author is in prison on the island of Patmos, cut off from the fellow-Christians to whom he is writing, and we may compare his book with some of the letters from totalitarian prisons and concentration camps, which have become famous in our own century of torture and bloodshed. Apocalyptic literature no longer seems so outlandish in this age of oppression and thought-control as it did to some of our politer and more civilised forefathers. 'Hold fast, do not betray your faith' is the message of John the Divine; and in the midst of what must have sometimes seemed to him and the small Christian communities to whom he was writing a hopeless, all-pervading darkness, he tells of the brilliant light that has shone on him from above, a light that no evil power on earth can quench.

The short hymns which punctuate Revelation – all of them acclamations or doxologies offered to God and to Jesus, the Lamb of God – are not to be read only as if they were so many earthly compositions arising out of particular human situations. In the context of John's vision, they are heard rather as snatches of the music of another world, that world where God reigns supreme in the Kingdom of love and is adored by all the myriads that surround Him. They recall Shakespeare's lovely lines from *The Merchant of Venice (V.i.54):*

> . . . look, how the floor of heaven
> Is there inlaid with patines of bright gold:
> There's not the smallest orb which thou behold'st

> But in his motion like an angel sings,
> Still quiring to the young-eyed cherubins;
> Such harmony is in immortal souls,
> But whilst this muddy vesture of decay
> Doth grossly close it in, we cannot hear it.

Every one of the heavenly hymns is **'a new song'** (Rev. 5. 9): that is, although in a sense the theme is always the same, the transport of love which animates it keeps it from any sense of staleness – just as the notion of 'eternity' is to be distinguished from that of time and of its infinite duration which to us would seem inconceivably tedious. It is of another order, another quality, from that which our finite minds and hearts can grasp. But were it to be *altogether* of another order, of course, it could never be translated into earthly language at all – nor could we sing this canticle! It is **'the Lamb who was slain'** who forms the bridge between heaven and earth. As Jeremy Taylor so beautifully said:

> Jesus was like a rainbow which God set in the clouds as a sacrament, to confirm a promise and establish a grace. He was half made of the glories of the light and half of the moisture of a cloud. In his best days he was but half triumph and half sorrow.
>
> (The Faith and Patience of the Saints)

Thus it comes about that in Revelation it is Jesus who unlocks the book which holds the mystery of creation and its destiny (Rev. 5. 7). The God who created all things is also the God who has given us our redemption through the Lamb who takes away the sin of the world. (Jn 1. 29)

Yet however exalted the vision of John may be, it is important to emphasise that he did not regard it as a private vision to be hugged to himself. On the contrary, he is impelled to communicate it as fully as possible. He is writing to actual churches in Asia Minor, no doubt to people whom he could name if he wished, with words both of warning and encouragement. For the Lamb seen in the heavenly places is that same Jesus who in the days of his flesh gathered round him a small company of people; and that company has been increasing ever since he died on Calvary and rose again, and will increase until the end about which John is prophesying. When we think of the (by modern standards) insignificant nature of the Church in John's day, some seventy years after Jesus' earthly life, we may marvel at the claim that disciples have been called 'from every race and language, from every people and nation' to be **'a kingdom of priests to stand and serve before our God'**. Yet such is the faith of the New Testament writers generally. We find it in a famous passage of Peter (I Pet. 2. 9–10) and repeatedly in the letters of Paul. And to look at that amazing combination of small, struggling, often tempted congregations with the cosmic vision of glorious destiny which surrounds and awaits them can give an altogether new perspective, some two thousand years later, to Christian churches that are in much the same state. **'A kingdom of priests'**: it is a phrase that strikes rather strangely on a modern ear – perhaps ominously to those who call themselves 'lay people' and think that one or two priests are enough, let alone a kingdom of them! But of course to the author there is no such distinction. *All* Christ's people, of whatever degree and from whatever part of the world, together form a single kingdom here and now (this is the vision behind all that we now call 'ecumenism'); and it is because we share in the life and mission of Christ himself, the Anointed One, both king and priest, and because of that alone, that we have together received this royal and priestly title – not just for our own honour, but that we may represent and serve all humanity as Christ himself has done.

In John's vision there are other things – pictures of divine wrath and vengeance – which are bound to make many a Christian uneasy, magnificent 'theatre' though they may be. Can we recognise in them the features of the Father who so loved the world, or the Son who came to seek and save the lost? Yet from this book written out of great suffering we take away above all the picture of the kingdom which is unshakeable (Heb. 12.28) and a kingdom which bridges heaven and earth. As citizens of that kingdom we are already able to hear something of the music of heaven, despite 'our muddy vesture of decay', because Christ enables us to hear it. It may break suddenly upon us with the triumphant sound of 'Worthy is the Lamb' in Handel's *Messiah* – or it may be a faint sound, just audible and no more. But whenever it comes, we thank God and take fresh courage, knowing that we are never alone, knowing that our worship and our pilgrimage alike are sustained by, taken into, the song of angels and archangels and the whole company of heaven.

7
TE DEUM LAUDAMUS

'We praise Thee, O God. . .'

It has long been the custom in our Church to conclude great services of celebration and thanksgiving – national, diocesan, parochial – with the singing of this canticle as a kind of triumphant shout, and many composers have treated it in that spirit. No doubt it is characteristic of human nature that we should have done our best to appropriate to our own glory a hymn which was intended to proclaim the glory of God, Father, Son and Holy Spirit. For no canticle is more sublimely God-directed than this one. For this purpose it brings 'on stage' like an immense cast at the end of a play, the hosts both of heaven and of earth; and we should picture them not as ranged in a straight line to take their bow, but rather in the manner of an *ikonostasis*, the screen in an Orthodox church, where row upon row of figures, human and angelic, ascend almost out of sight to the heaven of their aspiring praise. So at the Liturgy we sing –

> Rank on rank the host of heaven spreads its vanguard on the way.
> As the Light of light descendeth from the realms of endless day.
> That the powers of hell may vanish as the darkness clears away.
> At his feet the six-winged Seraph; Cherubim with sleepless eye
> Veil their faces to the Presence, as with ceaseless voice they cry
> 'Alleluya, Alleluya, Alleluya, Lord most high.'
>
> (Liturgy of St James, tr. G. Moultrie)

There is something pleasing in the thought that the *Te Deum*, perhaps the most famous and enduring of all Christian hymns, was written by a man of whom no one else has heard (at least, he may be a well-known bishop in the history of Yugoslavia, but certainly not in the West). For the old legend that this canticle was spontaneously produced, verse and verse about, by St Ambrose and St Augustine after the former had baptised the latter, may be confidently put down to the ancient love – so confusing to accurate-minded modern people – of attaching notable writings to notable figures. The real author is thought by most scholars to be one Niceta, bishop of Remesiana, in what is now Yugoslavia, from about 370–414 A.D. That was the age of the creeds and the basilicas, many of the latter bearing in their domes the figure of Christ the Pantocrator, or ruler of the universe. And for thousands of Christians today who may never have been to the Mediterranean countries to see these mighty churches, and who may remain ignorant of the fierce controversies surrounding the Creeds of Chalcedon and Constantinople, this hymn remains the greatest monument of that age, translating doctrine into the highest art of worship.

We may begin with a simplification. The closing section, from 'O Lord, save thy people. . .' to the end, does not form part of the original hymn, but is tacked on to it as what is called a *capitellum*, or series of short prayers to be said antiphonally. This is not at all to decry the beauty of these eight verses (which have often been included in choral settings, but would probably sound best to plainsong). They are so much better than the series of versicles and responses in Prayer Book Matins and Evensong, that it is a pity the churches in Britain did not follow the good example of the Episcopal Church in the U.S.A. and adopt them instead. However, we need think of them no more as belonging to the *Te Deum* proper. The canticle then ends, not quietly, but on a sublime note: 'make them to be rewarded ('numbered' is the English version of an ancient misprint in the Latin) with thy saints in glory everlasting'.

* * *

The hymn which remains consists of two parts, or acclamations as we have learned to call them. The first, down to 'also the Holy Ghost, the Comforter' is addressed to God in the fulness of his majesty, the Holy and Undivided Trinity. Its opening words really mean 'we praise thee as God. . .', but although the modern version found in the A.S.B. 'You are God and we praise you' is therefore more accurate, it cannot avoid sounding rather clumsy and even ridiculous. The crispness of the old version keeps the rhythm – we might almost say 'the swing' – of this whole section wonderfully well. Yet in the last verse we may concede a point to the A.S.B.; for 'the Holy Ghost, the Comforter' does not convey much to modern ears and 'the Holy Spirit, advocate and guide' seems a great improvement.

We have already noted in the Book of Revelation the swelling chorus in which the adoring hosts of heaven are joined by the Church on earth: as in John Milton's great lines –

> O may we soon again renew that song
> And keep in tune with heaven, till God ere long
> To his celestial consort us unite
> To live with him and sing in endless morn of light!
> (At a Solemn Musick)

What may kindle our imagination here is that already, only some four hundred years after Jesus' earthly life, the author could speak of 'the Holy Church throughout all the world', and doubtless think of apostles, prophets and martyrs by name. How vastly has the scale of that conception, and the number of the saints increased by our own day! The recent revision of the Church's Calendar in the A.S.B. has seen the addition of the names of many men and women, and has introduced a whole new geographical category, so that we now remember saints of Asia, Africa, the Americas and the Pacific, as well as those of nearer home. The *Te Deum* can truly be called an ever-expanding chorus of praise, as one generation succeeds another.

In the second part of this canticle, after so many different human figures, one comes into focus: that of Jesus Christ himself. In eight short verses, what Christians have called the Incarnation and the Atonement are celebrated with a marvellous simplicity, and the same points which are contained in the Creeds are found here also: his birth, his death, his sitting with the Father, his coming again. 'Who for us men and for our salvation came down from heaven. . .': all this was undertaken for our sakes, it was for our liberation that the way from Bethlehem to Calvary was trodden, and now the door of the Kingdom of heaven stands open for us. It is the same Christ who has come to be our Saviour, who will in the end be our Judge; and therefore it behoves us to pray, and to keep praying, that his outpouring of himself in sacrifice may not have been in vain. This is a prayer not prompted by fear, but rather by love of him who first loved us, and a recollection of the immense cost of that love.

> **Blessed be the Lord day by day, who bears us as his burden: he is the God of our deliverance.(Ps. 68.19)**

The section ends as it began, with the word 'glory'. The glory of the Father is surrounded by that 'light inaccessible' which is reflected in the works of the greatest artists and poets of humanity, and which yet remains beyond our imagining. Yet the King of Glory is also the Son of Man, the head of all creation. In him we touched the hems of the divine glory – and not just, as might be thought, on the Mount of Transfiguration but supremely (as St John insists) on the Mount of Crucifixion, the place of apparent waste, cruelty and shame. **'Father, the hour has come'** said Jesus at the Last Supper. **'Glorify thy Son, that the Son may glorify thee'** (Jn. 17.1). The words spoken on the eve of betrayal and self-sacrifice assure us that there is nothing remote or frigid about the glory of the Father, but that it is in truth a synonym for the heart of love, and that Jesus is (in the lovely words of Prudentius' hymn which we sing at Christmas)

Of the Father's heart begotten
  Ere the world from chaos rose.

We may not say, therefore, that it is only in the most beautiful moments of our lives, as we deem them, that the glory of God envelops us. That a woman could declare, as in a recent broadcast, that she has learnt the loving presence of God with her through the upbringing of a helplessly handicapped child to manhood: such paradoxes in life tell us otherwise. The glory surrounding Christ is not one which is divorced from the daily struggles in which we are involved, not one which is ignorant of our limitations, our sufferings and, indeed, our sins and failures. Were it so, no meaning could be attached to the prayer, 'make us to be rewarded with thy saints in glory everlasting'. But now our true home and destiny lie within that glory, to be with Christ. Therefore at the end of our writings, our singing, our thinking, we come back to the refrain:

Glory be to the Father and to the Son and to the Holy Spirit; as it was in the beginning, is now, and ever shall be, world without end. Amen.